PRACTICAL
HAPPINESS

PRACTICAL
HAPPINESS

Simple techniques for bringing
positivity, joy and balance
into everyday life

KIM DAVIES

LORENZ BOOKS

contents

What is happiness anyway?

Everyone wants to be happy – but what do we mean by happiness? Thinkers and artists down the centuries have tried to sum it up. 'Happiness lies in the joy of achievement and the thrill of creative effort,' said Franklin D. Roosevelt. 'There is only one happiness in this life: to love and be loved,' was the novelist George Sand's contribution, while Nobel prizewinner Albert Schweitzer offered: 'Happiness is nothing more than good health and a bad memory.'

Many psychologists have been inspired by the views of the Greek philosopher Aristotle, who believed that happiness is the whole purpose of human life. In his view, happiness consisted of two ingredients. One is *hedonia*, or pleasure. The other is *eudaimonia*, a more complex idea that is best translated with the phrase 'a life well lived'. Modern research suggests that our happiness really does depends on a balance between everyday moments of joy on the one hand, and a deep sense of meaning in our lives on the

The greatest discovery of any generation is that a human can alter his life by altering his attitude.

WILLIAM JAMES

other. And it is no good doubling up on one half of the equation. A life devoted entirely to gratification, say, soon becomes jaded and empty, as many a bored and miserable millionaire can attest.

The American constitution declares that everyone has a right to 'the pursuit of happiness'. That's certainly true, but the pursuit should never become single-minded. There are studies to show that, paradoxically, focusing too much on your own happiness is a self-defeating process that can increase feelings of disappointment and discontent. Happiness, it has rightly been said, like life, is something that happens while you are busy doing other things.

No life is blessed throughout with good fortune. All of us face setbacks and sorrows. It follows that, if we want to be truly happy we cannot depend solely on external factors, on things going well. We have to look within. That means that happiness is not just a state of mind, it is an attitude we can take, as well as something we can action. As the pioneering psychologist William James once said: 'The good we do today becomes the happiness of tomorrow.'

Happiness is a continuous process rather than a goal – a journey rather than a destination, in other words. The book you are holding is a kind of guide, one that includes lots of routes and byways. It draws on views and ideas from all kinds of places – spiritual thinkers, modern science and research – and it presents the information in a practical, helpful way. As with any guidebook, you can read right through, go straight to the chapters that seem relevant to your path, or open the book at random just to see what you might find.

Building our resilience and ability to cope when things do go wrong is as important as learning to appreciate the things that do go right. Before you begin to explore your own happiness journey, the following pages suggest a handful of instant ways to boost the joy quotient in your life, so you can get started straight away.

Start here: happiness boosters

If you are looking for greater happiness in life, then the good news is that there actually are some quick fixes, easy ways to give yourself a momentary boost. Here are a few science-backed ways that are (almost) guaranteed to lift you up. Most of us realise when we stop to think about it that it is the small things that give us most joy – meeting up with friends or enjoying a cup of good coffee, say. We can boost our happiness very easily by lingering over and savouring things.

1. Be here now The swiftest way to make yourself feel better is simply to stop what you are doing, take a deep breath, and allow yourself to notice what you can see, hear, touch, smell, and taste. Fully engaging in the moment is an instant stress-reliever, and can connect us immediately with feelings of appreciation and calm.

2. Walk on Going for a stroll is a great happiness habit, as well as an effective way to feel good right now. Take your strides long, swing your arms, and hold your head high. In one US study, people who walked this way for three minutes felt significantly happier than those who took small shuffling steps and looked down.

3. Have a cuppa Drinking tea has been shown to have an instantly soothing effect, because it helps boost levels of the feelgood brain chemicals dopamine and serotonin. While you are drinking your tea, focus fully: enjoy the aroma and the warmth of the cup on your hands as well as the taste.

4. Peel a clementine Smells can stir an emotion more effectively than sights or sounds. One study has found that the citrus scent of clementine has an immediately uplifting effect on mood. Lilies, meanwhile, contain a chemical compound called linalool that promotes calm.

5. Speed think Set yourself a challenge such as naming as many of your primary school teachers as you can; or come up with five unusual uses for a common household object such as a colander or sieve. Rapid-fire thinking such as this can enhance feelings of elation and promote creativity, say researchers at Harvard and Princeton.

6. Enjoy a real tweet A study conducted at King's College, London, found that listening to birdsong can boost your mood. So go outside, find a tree to sit under, and listen to the birds. You may notice the song change as the bird gets used to your presence. It's fascinating as well as life-affirming.

7. Be open to melody Music bypasses your reasoning brain and goes straight to your emotions. That is why it can move us so profoundly. In a few words, happy music makes you happy, and according to Canadian researchers, it also allows us to access positive memories – which is another source of joy. Singing out loud has a similar effect, because it gets oxygen into the body, and releases endorphins into the system.

8. And smile... The very act of smiling can put you in a better mood. Smiling triggers a reaction in the brain, causing it to release dopamine and serotonin, which make you feel happier, a circular reaction.

THE *happiness* HABIT

Take a look at the basic building blocks of well-being: good sleep, exercise, diet and more. Chances are that if one of these is under par, your happiness will be affected.

Happiness habit one: Start well

Embrace the knowledge that each morning contains the promise of a happy day. Your morning routine sets the tone for all that follows, so it makes sense to start as you want to go on. Use these simple tips to make your mornings happier.

Be inspired The first thing that you do in the morning should give you joy – not least because this will give you a good reason to jump out of bed. Allow yourself at least 20 minutes longer than you need to get ready for your day, so you can make time for something that feels truly enjoyable – yoga, meditating, writing a journal, lingering over a good cup of coffee, whatever pleases you.

Stop the snooze If you use an alarm clock, put it across the room so that you have to get up to turn it off. Hitting snooze and falling back to sleep means that you start a new sleep cycle and the chances are that you'll be in an even deeper sleep next time the alarm

goes off. If you feel underslept and grumpy each morning, it could be that the alarm is set at a time when you are usually in a deep sleep. Experiment by setting it to go off a few minutes later or earlier, to assess if that improves your mood. And choose a melodic sound rather than a siren or clanging bell.

Stretch out The American Council on Exercise recommends doing a few gentle stretches when you get out of bed in the morning. Stretching increases blood flow to the muscles (which are naturally stiff after a night in bed) and also to the brain, helping to get your body and your mind in gear for the day ahead.

Make your bed This is the advice from naval admiral William H. McRaven, who served as commander of the US Special Forces. Making your bed as soon as you get up means the day starts with a mini-accomplishment that not only makes you feel good, it helps inspire you to achieve the next. It's also is a reminder that the little things in life matter.

Embrace the light Get outside early if you can – morning light helps trigger the body's production of melatonin, which has an antidepressant effect. Or at least open up your curtains or blinds.

Have a cold shower A morning blast of cold water can leave you feeling invigorated and trigger the release of feel-good endorphins. Research shows that regular cold showers can help alleviate depression. If a full-on cold shower is too much, start with cool.

When you arise in the morning, think of what a precious privilege it is to be alive – to breathe, to think, to enjoy, to love.

MARCUS AURELIUS

Happiness habit two: Spend time outdoors

The 19th-century American essayist Henry David Thoreau wrote that 'We can never have enough of Nature… take long walks in stormy weather or through deep snows in the fields and woods if you would keep your spirits up.'

Thoreau lived alone in the wilderness for two years, and modern scientific evidence confirms what he learned the hard way: if you want to feel happier, enjoy nature. Study after study has shown that immersing oneself in nature bestows many psychological benefits such as lowering stress and boosting feelings of joy and inspiration.

Our urban way of life leaves us increasingly out of touch with nature. Most of us spend the majority of our time indoors and even when we are out we don't actively engage with natural world. And yet we are instinctively happier in nature, where everything moves at its own pace, where we experience natural diversity and beauty, and where we are open to our connection with the earth around us. Our species evolved in open grassland under the warmth of the sun, after all; no wonder we feel at home outdoors.

Being close to a natural environment has a positive effect. Several studies, including one from the University of Exeter, have found that people who moved to a greener location experienced an immediate and long-lasting improvement in well-being. And separate studies have found that looking out of the window on to a natural scene, or having flowers and houseplants in your home – even simply looking at pictures of natural scenes – can boost your everyday mood as well as enhancing your living space.

> *All nature has a feeling: woods,*
> *fields, brooks*
> *Are life eternal: and in silence they*
> *Speak happiness beyond the*
> *reach of books…*
>
> JOHN CLARE

A daily fix of nature

Challenge yourself over the course of a month to get outdoors and actively enjoy the natural world for at least 15 minutes. Researchers at the University of Derby analysed data from the UK's Wildlife Trust, and found that even that short exposure to nature can lead to increased feelings of happiness and well-being. So…

✳ Go for a hike or a challenging walk: climb a mountain or follow a nature trail (or if these are not available, the local park).

✳ Stroll barefoot through grass or over sand.

✳ Encourage wildlife in your own outdoor space by putting up a bird feeder, or planting bee-friendly flowers in a border or window box. Spend time each day, watching creatures come and go.

✳ Get wet: go for a swim in the sea, or go out for a stroll in the rain.

✳ Make an appointment with the sunrise or sunset: few natural experiences are more inspiring and calming, and this one happens every single day.

✳ Lie down out in the open: watch the scudding clouds, have a nap, or stare at the spangled night sky.

I only went out for a walk and finally concluded to stay out till sundown, for going out, I found, was really going in.

JOHN MUIR

Forest bathing

In Japan the healing atmosphere of trees has been turned into a form of therapy – shinrin-yoku, or forest bathing. Many studies confirm that being around trees for as little as 15 minutes can reduce anxiety and promote feelings of well-being. Try this version of forest bathing, either in woodland or in your local park.

1. Go for a walk, leaving your phone behind you or at least putting it on silent. If you are with other people, agree not to talk as you walk. Walk slowly, and as you do so make a conscious attempt to notice and appreciate the surroundings: breathe in deeply, taking in the aromas of the trees, and observing the many different greens and browns of the trees and plants. Wander wherever feels right rather than trying to follow a particular path or reach a certain point.

2. If something catches your attention, pause and really focus on it. Notice the small details, the slow progress of an insect, a patch of dappled sunlight on the ground.

A family affair

The present generation of children spends less time out of doors than any previous one. Giving children and teens more 'green time' is an important way to build their resilience and reduce stress. There is evidence that playing in green settings or going for a walk in a natural environment has a positive effect on children's attention span.

Prioritising nature-time is also important for older and less mobile people, who may have restricted access to the countryside. Helping them to visit and enabling them to enjoy fresh and natural surroundings is a kindness.

Engage your sense of touch – brushing a leaf or flower with your fingertips, or resting your palms on the rough bark of a tree.

3. Find somewhere to sit and lie down. Tune into the sounds of the forests – birdsong, passing breezes, the rustle and murmur of the trees themselves. Allow yourself to be in this healing space for as long as feels

pleasurable to you, then slowly make your way back to your starting point.

4. Try coming to the same place regularly, to walk and just 'be'. This can increase your sense of connection with nature, as you develop a sense of belonging here, and start to notice how the environment changes over time and with the seasons.

Happiness habit three: Eat for joy

There's no doubt that what you eat affects the way you feel. Some foods give an instant uplift while the essential nutrients in a healthy diet help regulate your moods. The general rule is: keep it natural.

A simpler way

We eat fewer vegetables and much less fish than our grandparents, and a lot more packaged food. And as our diet has shifted, there has been a corresponding rise in mental health conditions. It's thought that industrial farming, junk food and processed meals all contribute to a lower level of nutrients in our organs, the brain included. Here are five easy ways to eat for happiness.

Chew more plants If you do nothing else, simply increasing the amount of fruit and vegetables that you eat could impact on your happiness. An Australian survey of 12,000 people found that happiness levels increased with each extra serving eaten during the day.

Eat clean The fewer junk foods in your diet, the better. They are full of 'empty' calories, filling you up and leaving you with a craving for more, without providing the nutrients we need for health and happiness. Aim to cook from natural ingredients wherever possible, and cut back on takeaways, ready meals, shop-bought cakes and biscuits. A diet high

in processed foods and trans fats is linked with depression and mood swings. But the good news is that the fewer junk foods you eat, the less you crave them, so a healthy diet gets easier if you stick with it.

Be whole Processed grains, such as white pasta, bread and white rice, and junk foods, cause a spike in your blood sugar that gives you a quick burst of energy but the corresponding drop leaves you feeling tired and low. Brown rice and wholemeal bread or pasta releases energy slowly, which helps balance your mood.

Up the fish Omega-3 oils – found in olive oil and in oily fish such as salmon, mackerel and sardines – seem to play a significant part in promoting optimal functioning of the parts of the brain involved in motivation and regulating emotions.

Go for B A lack of B vitamins has been linked to depression, so make sure foods rich in Vitamin B are present in your diet: meat and poultry, eggs, nuts, soya beans, bananas, leafy green vegetables. Another important nutrient is iron, found in red meat, egg yolk, green leafy veg, nuts and pulses.

Five quick fixes

Adding a few healthy foods to a bad diet won't make you magically happier, but there are plenty of foods that can give you a quick mood boost.

* Eat a banana or two to increase levels of potassium, which helps us utilise feel-good serotonin.

* Add chilli to your food – it promotes the release of endorphins.

* Eat a small amount of good quality dark chocolate, with 70 percent cacao. It reduces stress and boosts mood.

* A cup of tea or coffee contains caffeine that will give you an instant lift, but leave plenty of time for the caffeine to leave your system before bedtime.

* Drink water. Even mild dehydration can lead to mood swings, irritation and fatigue.

Make time for food

How you eat matters as much as what you eat. Treat food with respect and cherish the time you spend eating. For instance, slowing down and savouring your food will help you digest it properly – and also allows the brain time to recognise when you are full.

Take a tip from Buddhist monks and 'eat when you are eating' – in other words, don't try to eat while you are doing something else, such as watching TV or working or checking your phone…

The wonderful exception to this rule is the universal practice of eating with others. Sharing food has always been a way of fostering connection and bonding: this is true of every culture from the beginning of human history – and earlier. Studies show that even chimpanzees experience elevated levels of the love hormone oxytocin after sharing food. And it is proven that sharing family meals helps to promote empathy in children. They are also a great way of touching base with partners, teenagers, family members or anyone else you might live with. Intriguingly, meals taken at home seem to have a more beneficial effect than eating out. One study involving 160 women found that they reported feeling happier and less stressed after eating at home, and they also ate more healthily there.

Try this: Liberate the table. Rather than use your table as a dumping ground for papers and other paraphernalia, keep it clear and lay it for meals. Make it an appealing space to gather round, to promote a feeling of pleasure and communality.

Happiness habit four: Get moving

Exercise is an excellent way to boost your well-being. A study by the University of Vermont discovered that 20 minutes' activity can lead to an improvement in mood lasting 12 hours. And regular exercise has been shown to be so good for mental health that doctors prescribe it to people with depression and anxiety.

Exercise has not only a direct effect on your mental well-being, but it improves other happiness-inducing aspects of lifestyle such as good sleep. It promotes the flow of blood to the brain, which encourages clear thinking and decision-making – which in turn are likely to make you happier. It can be a good distraction from upsetting thoughts, and meeting exercise-related goals can help boost your sense of achievement and your self-esteem.

Making moves

If you just want to feel a bit happier it seems almost any exercise will do: 10 minutes a week could be enough to affect your mood

according to one review of the evidence. But the general prescription for both physical and mental health says that each week we should do several sessions amounting to at least 2.5 hours of moderate exercise (brisk walking or swimming, say) – or a lesser amount of more vigorous exercise. A Finnish study found that people who exercised two or three times a week experienced less depression, anger and stress than those who didn't.

Does this mean you should force yourself to exercise even if you dislike it? Yes and no. Many people find that once they make exercise a habit, they grow to like it – but others don't. Clearly, keeping fit can make you happier, but forcing yourself to do anything you dislike seems counter-productive. So, it is better in this case to apply some creativity to your approach, and come up with ways to be active that do feel enjoyable – hiking rather than going to the gym, aqua fitness classes rather than swimming, dance rather than aerobics, going horse riding rather than running round a track… Or just walk – it's the simplest and most obvious form of exercise, it cannot help but do you good, and it is easy to increase the benefits just by walking faster and pumping your arms.

As with any exercise regime, it's worth setting the bar quite low at first – stick to short workouts and go gently. This helps you exercise safely and it also makes it more likely you will continue. Here are some tips for getting going, and keeping going.

1. Give yourself an achievable goal – say, walking for 10 minutes a day twice a week.

2. Tick off your achievements – acknowledging your successes helps you stay motivated.

3. Know why you are exercising – write down your key reasons for exercise on a piece of paper and stick it somewhere you will see it often.

4. Pair up with a friend – ideally one who is the same fitness level as you. Having an exercise buddy makes it much less likely that you will just give it a miss.

5. Do it outdoors – the UK's University of Essex suggests that outdoor workouts have greater psychological benefits than indoor exercising.

6. Listen to music or podcast – because this can make exercising feel more productive and fun.

7. Find a time that is easy – first thing in the morning is good, because it starts the day off with a win.

8. Clear the obstacles – sort out your kit the night before to make it as easy as possible to exercise in the morning.

Happiness habit five: Downgrade the digital

Technology has revolutionised our lives, but it isn't necessarily making us happier. We are beginning to see that our connectedness can take a form that is very similar to addiction. Most of us agree that we – and our children – would feel more content and in control if we limited our use of smartphones and the like. And the positive news is that we can.

Our smartphones have so many functions – GPS, calendar, messaging, emails – that we struggle to go a day without them. For many of us, checking our phone is the first thing we do when we wake up and the last thing we do at night. According to one survey, the average user spends around four hours a day on their phone – which, when you come to think about it, amounts to a quarter of our waking hours. For many of us, technology has become a dependence, one that undermines our happiness and cause us stress and guilt.

Track it

Studies show that most of us underestimate the amount of time we spend on our devices. If you want to reduce your digital addition, then the first step is to track how

much you use technology. If you have teens or younger children, this is a good thing to do together as a family.

1. Make a list of all your devices Then spend at least one weekday and the whole of a weekend keeping a tally of how often you use them, as well as for what purpose. You might like to install a free app such as Moment to help you.

2. Work out what you want to use your phone for There's no doubt that smartphones offer many benefits. What are the positives of yours? And what are the negatives? It can help to write down the apps that you want to keep and the ones that you want to delete or use less.

3. What do you want to do with the time you are going to save? Play the guitar? Read books? Learn Spanish? Cook more? Think about how you could make this easier for yourself: if, for example, you want to read more, where can you leave your book so that it catches your eye? if you want to cook more, find some interesting new recipes to try.

How men undervalue the power of simplicity! But it is the real key to the heart.

WILLIAM WORDSWORTH

Change your phone habit

1. Declutter your phone Delete the apps that pointlessly eat up your time – games, social media, and so on. If you do want to keep using them, have them on another device that is less readily available – for example, access Facebook from a home computer, rather than your phone.

2. Disable notifications Allowing apps to send you notifications creates a false sense of urgency, which is stressful. Notification or not, it can all wait. Remember you can always re-enable notifications for particular apps if you find that you really need them.

3. Make your phone less distracting Organise your home screen so that only the apps you really want to use are visible; put the others in folders in interior screens.

4. Make yourself think Try putting a message to yourself on your lock screen: 'DO YOU NEED TO USE THE PHONE?', for example.

5. Use other kit. The amazing multi-functionality of our phones is what keeps us hooked. So go analogue from time to time. Wear a watch, consult a map, write with pen and paper. And commit to not using tech when you are spending time outdoors.

Change your habits

Generally speaking it's easier to change one habit at a time. So start with one of the suggestions below, and do it for two to three days. Then add another one into the mix – you can work in the order they are listed here, or mix it up. Expect to apply some self-discipline.

1. Clear the table Have a no-phones-at-the-table rule for mealtimes. This is particularly useful if you live with teenagers and want to ringfence some family time. Leave them in another room, or well away from the table, on silent.

2. UnGoogle Most of us turn to Google (or Bing!) when there's a trivial fact we can't

remember in conversation. Ban yourself from doing this for non-essentials and use your mind instead – this is easier if you don't keep your phone to hand the whole time.

3. Have no-phone zones Keep devices out of bedrooms – which will certainly help your sleep. Bathrooms too: no watching movies in the bath. Instead, enjoy a peaceful soak. And if you need access to your phone, keep it further away than arm's length to stop you picking it up without thinking.

4. Keep eye contact Make it a rule to look people in the eye when you are in conversation – whether at home, out or at work. Put your phone away: a study by the University of Essex found that having a mobile phone visible made people seem less relatable and more negative even if they weren't using it.

5. Prioritise your children Most parents worry about their children's use of technology, but your own usage may be even more problematic: one study found that parents using smartphones while with their children were less attentive and felt less connected to them; another discovered that parents who said they were addicted to their smartphones were more likely to have children with behavioural problems. When you are with your kids (teens included), put the phone away.

6. Make an appointment Have a single set time to look at social media each day rather than continually checking it. Reduce the number of times you post, too – once instead of multiple times a day; twice a week instead of daily, for example.

7. Have a digi-holiday Put your devices away for half a day once a week – and take a full day off once a month. Let others know you are doing this so you are not worried about being out of contact. Once you get used to doing this, build up so that you can take a whole weekend off – it's blissful.

Happiness habit six: Sleep long and deep

Sleep is worth more than money when it comes to your happiness. That's not just a turn of phrase – it's statistically proven. A happiness index based on a poll of British adults found that well-rested people scored 15 points higher than those who were sleep-poor. By contrast, those who earned four times the salary gained only 2 extra points of happiness.

Anyone who has had a bad night's sleep knows that it makes you feel lousy – but the impact is much wider than that. If you are tired, then you are more likely to overeat, underperform, be irritable, and less likely to exercise, have sex, or socialise – all things that affect your happy mode. Over time, regular lack of sleep is linked to a host of mental health conditions, including depression and anxiety, as well as physical health issues. So the first step towards improving your sleep is acknowledging how much it matters. There are practical things you can do to help improve your sleep.

Prioritise your sleep

Despite the known benefits of a good night's sleep, it is often the first things we sacrifice when we are busy. Here are some ways to get the best of your rest.

Love your bedroom It's easier to drop off in a clean, uncluttered room that's dark, quiet and relatively cool. Keep anything to do with work or technology outside, and use your bedroom just for rest and intimacy. If noise disturbs you, get thicker curtains or wear earplugs. And replace your mattress if it's uncomfortable or old.

Release worry Find ways to switch off after work. If you are worrying in the evening, try writing down everything you are thinking about. Leave your notes well away from the bedroom. When a worry resurfaces, remind yourself it's spending the night in your journal so you don't have to ponder it now.

Watch the sleep stealers The caffeine in coffee (and tea and chocolate) can take seven hours to leave your system, so avoid these things from the afternoon onwards. Alcohol can help us relax and therefore drop off, but makes sleep fractured and less restful. As for

There is a time for many words and there is also a time for sleep.

HOMER

dinner, the advice is eat early then stick to light snacks later on. Your body will have time to digest properly, which is better for weight management as well.

Dim the lights Bright lights signal daytime to the brain. Use side lights and dimmer switchers to create a sleep-friendly ambience in your home an hour or two before bedtime.

Cut the tech The shining screens of smartphones likewise send wakeful signals to the brain – so stay off them for at least two hours before sleep. Use an alarm clock so you can leave your smartphone outside your bedroom. A review of more than 11 studies found that the sleep of teens and children was disrupted by the mere presence of a smartphone in their room – even if they weren't touching it!

Wind down If you are wired when you get into bed, it'll take you longer to drop off. Spend the hour before bedtime on activities that soothe the mind and relax the body: a warm bath, relaxation exercises or meditation,

listening to calming music, reading happy books. Make this your regular routine, so that the associations prime your body for sleep. And try to go to bed at the same time each night.

Sleep naked A study by the University of Amsterdam found that sleeping naked lowers your skin temperature, which helps to promote deep sleep and reduce the number of night wakings you have.

Follow the 20-minute rule The UK Sleep Council recommends that if you don't fall asleep within 20 minutes of turning out the light, get up and do some calming activity such as reading or listening to music instead.

Use the day What you do during the day has a big impact on your night-time sleep. In particular, exercise and getting plenty of daylight – both things that are good for your happiness – also help to set you up for a good sleep.

A well-spent day brings happy sleep.
LEONARDO DA VINCI

And relax...

Autogenic relaxation, a technique invented in the 1930s, is a great way to release physical tension and promote calmness of mind. You can use it in bed to help you drift off to sleep, or as a relaxation exercise at any time of day. As with any such technique, you will get better at it if you practise regularly. Try doing it twice a day for a couple of weeks.

1. Lie down in bed, or sit comfortably on a sofa or armchair, and close your eyes. Take a few deep breaths.

2. Focus your attention on your arms and say the following to yourself: 'My arms are heavy' six times, followed by 'My arms are warm' – again, six times. Try to say the phrase with conscious awareness each time, letting the words form slowly in your mind rather than rushing through them.

3. Switch to your legs and repeat the phrases for them. 'My legs are heavy, my legs are warm', six times.

4. Now tune into your heartbeat. Say the phrase 'My heartbeat is calm and regular', six times.

5. Bring your attention to your breathing: 'My breathing is calm and deep', six times.

6. Now focus on the belly: 'My belly is warm', six times.

7. Let your attention drift to your forehead: 'My forehead is cool', six times.

8. Allow your attention to encompass the whole body, saying 'My whole body is relaxed and comfortable', six times.

9. If you are in bed, just stay aware of the feeling of relaxation and comfort in your body as you allow yourself to drift off to sleep; otherwise, open the eyes and get up slowly.

A *meaningful* LIFE

A happy life is a purposeful life.
Purpose helps to sustain us through
times of difficulty, and provides a
thread of meaning.

Finding purpose

We all want to be happy. But ironically if we focus too narrowly on our search for happiness this can lead us to prioritise fleeting pleasures above the satisfaction of a meaningful life. Having a sense of purpose allows you to be more adaptable and resilient, to weather the natural ups and downs that life brings. Ultimately, purpose is what leads us to a deeper and more long-lasting contentment in life.

The Japanese have a word *ikagi* that can be roughly translated as 'reason for living' or 'thing you live by'. Ikagi is often described as the thing you get out of bed for – it's like the Western idea of passion, but also integrates values and skills and a sense of the everyday. Importantly, ikagi is not just about what one achieves but also incorporates the idea that one's actions should be carried out with care and attention. Thus it allows us to take true satisfaction in every step of the process. And it seems that having something

The mystery of human existence lies not in just staying alive, but in finding something to live for.

FYODOR DOSTOYEVSKY

to live for does in fact help us to live longer – a recent study of more than 70,000 Japanese people found that people with a strong purpose had greater longevity. The

concept of ikagi is central to the daily routine of the people of Okinawa, a region famous for having one of the highest incidences of centenarians in the world.

Creative people such as singers, artists and writers often have a strong ikagi, as do those with a sense of vocation – doctors, teachers, even some politicians. But although your purpose can be your paid work, it doesn't have to be. You could say that your ikagi is the thing you do that makes a difference in the world. For some people, that could be rescuing street-dogs or planting trees, creating art or great music. For others, it can be about making a family

function well, or perhaps being an active member of a religious community or group (there is another Japanese word *ittaiken*, which means taking satisfaction in a role). Your ikagi can be lifelong, or it may change at different stages.

How do you find your ikagi/purpose?

If your ikagi is not obvious to you, take a sheet of paper, and add the following headings to it:

1. My values – what matters to me
2. My joys – what gives me pleasure
3. My strengths – what I am good at

When you have written down your three headings, take a short time to reflect on each one in turn. When you begin to write, try not to filter or edit yourself. Be completely truthful: if you write something that causes you mentally to roll your eyes, or you notice tension arising in your body, then consider if you are writing about something you think you should enjoy or value rather than actually do. If so, put a line through it. It can help to think back to when you were a child: what mattered to you most, what did you do effortlessly and with real joy?

These are lists that you can return to again and again, so don't feel you need to complete them straight away. You may like to complete them over the course of a few days, allowing time for the answers to come to you.

When you feel ready to do so, look at your lists and consider which of your values, joys and strengths written there resonate most deeply with you. And then, is there something that connects all three? For example, it may be that you value truthfulness and honesty, love reading, and are good at writing – could being an author or researcher be your ikagi? Or perhaps you love to be outdoors, value being eco-friendly, and are brilliant at organising and fundraising

> *One's philosophy is not best expressed in words; it is expressed in the choices one makes.*
>
> ELEANOR ROOSEVELT

– could creating a community garden or working for an eco-charity be your ikagi?

But but but…

It may well be that your circumstances are difficult right now – perhaps you are working long hours, in a difficult relationship, struggling to make a living or – conversely – making a lot of money doing something that gains you respect but doesn't make you truly happy.

All these things can make the idea of ikagi seem like an indulgence. And while it is true that we may not be able to follow our passion *right now*, thinking about ikagi can be a way to kickstart the process of living in a happier and more worthwhile way in the future. Knowing what it is you do want can allow you to take small steps towards change, grasp opportunities when they present themselves, and think more deeply about what it is you currently prioritise in life. And of course, circumstances can change, opening up possibilities and allowing us to live in a way that truly suits and sustains us. Keep asking yourself these two questions: 'What do I really want?' and, 'What is stopping me from getting it?' When you keep questioning yourself in this way, you may begin to realise that the biggest block to developing greater purpose is not your circumstances but something in yourself.

The best possible self

Another way to work out what you really want, is to visualise yourself in the future, living the life that would fulfil and complete you. The 'best possible self' exercise, created by psychologist Laura King, can help you to explore your motivations and dreams in a way that feels both practical and inspiring. Feeling optimistic about the future is one way to boost feelings of happiness in the present, and it also helps to build self-awareness, which can help you live in a way more likely to promote contentment.

This is a writing exercise that takes about 20 minutes to complete. Find a notebook and a pen, and a comfortable place to sit.

1. Choose a time in the future – 5 years, 10 years, 20 years hence. Then close your eyes and imagine that everything has gone as well as it could and you have achieved all that you truly desire. Think about the different aspects of your life – family, home, work, study or knowledge, interests and health – as well as your personal qualities.

2. Now open your eyes and write as much as you can about your future self. Be as detailed as possible – for example, if you are imagining yourself living in a new home, be specific about its features – perhaps it has a garden, or a study where you work…

3. If you find yourself thinking about reasons why your future couldn't possibly match up to your dreams, or about past obstacles or setbacks, gently let these thoughts go and bring your attention back to the exercise.

4. Be as creative and expressive as you can. Don't get hung up on elegant handwriting or perfectly written sentences. Just allow the words to flow freely.

5. Keep writing for 20 minutes. It's fine to take a pause and return to visualising your future self living your dreams, if you need

more inspiration. At the end of the time, put down your pen and put the paper away. Do the same exercise for at least three days.

Writing about your future self in this positive way has been shown to promote clarity about goals, as well as boost confidence, well-being and optimism in the short term. It can also move you to act in accordance with your deepest values and desires, and act as a positive motivator in a very practical way, keeping your ultimate aims in mind.

Honour the future

Bear in mind your future self when making your decisions. See your future self as someone who is important to you – as important as your current self, as important as those dearest to you.

Goal setting

Having goals boosts our motivation, and keeps us interested in life. Studies show that people are happier when they are working towards a goal – and this seems to hold true even when they do not meet it. So a goal is not simply a pathway toward a happier life, it is an important part of feeling good about how we spend our time.

Our goals can be long-term, such as getting fit or raising a family or changing your career path, or they can be short-term: doing that yoga practice every day this week or leaving work on time each day. However having short-term goals also allows a sense of achievement that can boost our day-to-day happiness. If they form part of our larger goals, they can feed into our overarching

sense of purpose to life. Remember goals are not merely targets to be hit or missed, they are not a question of total success or total failure. Having goals is a beneficial end in itself.

Set long-term goals

Goal-setting is a skill. As the Greek philosopher Aristotle (and Mary Poppins) said: 'Well begun is half done'. Here's how to set good goals:

1. Identify your overall goal – what is it that you want to achieve? The ikagi and 'best possible self' exercises described should help you with creating that vision. Make sure that your goal is something you really want, rather than something you think you should want.

2. Break down your vision into a set of milestones – achievements that are specific and measurable.

3. Divide these milestones further and further, until you have a set of small achievable steps (short-term goals).

*Keep your eyes on the stars and
your feet on the ground.*

THEODORE ROOSEVELT

4. Consider how the steps and milestones make you feel. If you feel excited and happy, then write down your overall vision, your set of milestones, and your list of smaller steps in a journal. There's evidence that writing your goals down helps you achieve more, and it also gives you a concrete way of marking progress, which can help keep you motivated. If you feel weary and daunted, then consider why the process feels so unattractive. Is this vision really the one that motivates you?

5. Decide on your first step and give yourself a time in which to achieve it. Is there something you can do right now?

6. Have a weekly review of your vision, milestones and goals. Work these into your daily and weekly to-do lists. Try to think of obstacles before they come up, and plan ways to get round them.

7. Enjoy the process. Every time you achieve one of your steps or milestones, allow yourself to celebrate. Visible progress makes us feel good, and feeling good helps keep us motivated. But don't let failure to achieve a particular step deflect you from your overall goal. Allow your plan to guide your way, but don't focus on your ultimate vision to the extent that it impacts negatively on your day-to-day well-being.

8. Setting tough goals makes us feel happier than having easy ones – so long as they are in some way realistic.

Prioritising what matters

If you want to feel happier, you need to find ways to maximise the time and energy you spend on the things that give you pleasure or support your sense of purpose. That means minimising the time you spend on things that militate against your own happiness.

Set boundaries

It's common to put the needs of others before your own, but if we routinely neglect our own needs we can become overwhelmed, exhausted and resentful.

If you want to be happier, then you may need to be a bit ruthless about the way you spend your time. You are sure to know at least some people who like you to use your time to facilitate their needs, and you yourself may feel that the world is full of more important things than what you want. But acknowledge that your needs and your happiness matter as much as everyone

> *It's not enough to be busy; so are the ants. The question is: what are we busy about?*
>
> HENRY DAVID THOREAU

else's. Ask yourself who will put your needs, your dreams, your happiness first if you don't?

* Set boundaries. If you have friends that you regularly counsel for hours, or you do favours for, or you feel obliged to go out with every Friday even when you are tired, then make a personal commitment to recalibrate that relationship.

* Notice how you are feeling inside when someone asks you to do something. If it doesn't make you feel good, then don't do it.

* Be realistic about what you can and can't sensibly do.

* Get comfortable with guilt. If you like pleasing other people then you are going to feel bad when you disappoint them. Remind yourself that a little guilt is a good thing – it means that you are starting to set boundaries.

Exercise: how to say no

Saying no is one of the most useful skills you can learn in order to take control of your own life. We find it hard, because we like to be liked, but there are times when we have to do it anyway. It is not being negative if sometimes it is necessary to say no. Here is how to start.

Be clear, but brief Say straight away, 'I won't be able to do that', or 'No, but thanks for asking'.

Avoid excuses The more excuses you give the weaker your 'no' sounds – and the other person may well come up with a counter-argument that prolongs the conversation. Don't lie – apart from anything else, it's too easy to get caught out.

Depersonalise If appropriate, give a global reason – 'I never lend money to friends' rather than 'I don't want to lend to you', or 'I'm not able to take on any more commitments right now'.

Buy time If you aren't sure, an easy way to say no is to delay making a decision. If you say 'I'll get back to you on that' or 'I'll need to think about it', you avoid making an immediate commitment and so give yourself a chance to consider what you want. But don't avoid saying no when you need to.

Don't ask for approval The other person doesn't have to like or agree with your refusal. We often agree to all sorts of things because we worry about what will happen if we don't. The absolute key to doing what you want is to accept that sometimes there will be consequences – the person may be annoyed, or not ask you next time – and that's okay.

Urgent vs important

Being busy can become a state of mind, so that even when things aren't that pressing, we operate as if they are. Most of us are vulnerable to a kind of illusion of busyness, especially nowadays when we are constantly contactable and liable to be interrupted at any given moment. That kind of busyness puts us in a reactive mode, being buffeted from one task to the next, so that we lose sight of long-term goals and dreams. Drop the busy-busy-busy attitude; accept the fact that you are not going to be able to do everything; delegate or ignore certain tasks and demands; and make space for things that give you true pleasure or align with your sense of purpose.

Dwight Eisenhower, war leader and US president, once said: 'I have two kinds of problems, the urgent and the important. The urgent are not important, and the important are never urgent.' There's a productivity technique based on this quote, popularised by American speaker and author Steven

> *Beware the barrenness of a busy life.*
> SOCRATES

Covey. It involves categorising your activities into the groups shown in the box below.

The trick is to stay on the top half of the matrix as much as possible. Things that are urgent and important need to be done straight away; things that are important but not urgent are generally the things that have most effect on your sense of happiness, but are easy to let slide in favour of the urgent and unimportant. So they need to be scheduled in and prioritised once the urgent and important have been taken care of.

Have a daily to-do list

Listing what you want to do in a day helps you to prioritise what really matters rather than allowing your time to be frittered away

Prioritise your tasks

Urgent and important	Important and not urgent
deadlines	self-care
medical emergencies	goals and dreams
family issues	relationships
Urgent and not important	Not important and not urgent
phone calls	social media
interruptions	watching TV
unexpected visitors	procrastination of all sorts

or controlled by one seeming emergency after another. Write it the evening before, bearing the Eisenhower matrix in mind. Ask yourself these questions:

✳ What is the one thing I can do tomorrow that will give me a true sense of accomplishment? *This is the first thing you should do (genuine emergencies aside).*

✳ What will give me pleasure? *By scheduling in joy, you will have something to look forward to and support your well-being.*

Leave white spaces

Keep the rest of your to-do list realistic. If your list is too long to manage, imagine that you are at the end of the day and have let a few things slide – why don't you cross these things off the list now?

Cramming your day with so much that you rush from one thing to the next is stressful – and it leaves no time for joy. Intentionally create blank spaces in your schedule, empty time that you can use to check in with yourself, breathe, doodle, rest, restore, enjoy and allow for creative thinking.

If you have a very crowded life, write down all your weekly and monthly commitments. Ask yourself which you could let go without jeopardising your overall goals. Start by de-committing to at least one thing.

Purpose at work

We spend most of our waking hours at work, and our jobs play a major part in how satisfied we feel generally. In an ideal world, your work will be an expression of your values and overall purpose in life – your ikagi. But even if your job does not feel like that, there are ways to find meaning and happiness at work.

Work is not just a source of financial security. It can be a place where we feel fulfilled and productive, somewhere that we can build positive relationships. It can be a well of affirmation and accomplishment, which builds self-esteem and empowerment. And it can be the bedrock of our personal status and our hopes, the means by which we build a better future for us and those we love.

However, the reality of work can feel very different. A worldwide study carried out by Gallup found that only about a third of Americans felt actively engaged and enthusiastic about their work – meaning almost two-thirds were either not engaged, or were actively disengaged and unenthusiastic about what they did for a living. And Americans scored much higher than workers in other parts of the world, including Europe – the global figure for active engagement at work was just 13 percent.

Job crafting

If you don't feel happy at work, then your instinct may be to look elsewhere. But it's worth looking to see whether you can

improve your current job first. Research by the University of Michigan showed that it is possible to develop passion for a job, even when it is not your ideal one. The researchers found that most of us believe we need to find the perfect 'fit' between our jobs and our values (the researchers called this group 'fit theorists'). Others believe you can develop a passion for a job even if it isn't exactly what you want to do ('develop theorists'). The study found that 'fit theorists' were more likely to say they felt well-suited to their job when they started it, but there was little difference between 'fit theorists' and 'develop theorists' when it came to current satisfaction at work.

As part of her research into how people find meaning at work, Professor Amy Wrzesniewski, from Yale School of Management, interviewed hospital cleaners. While many of those she interviewed found their cleaning work unsatisfying, others had a much more inspiring attitude towards what they did – seeing themselves as creating a healing environment or as helping ill people get well. Interestingly, the cleaners who felt positive about their work were often taking tasks in addition to those they were paid for. That is, they found fulfilment in building relationships with patients, engaging with their visitors, even changing the cleaning products they used depending on individual patient's preferences. Wrzesniewski dubbed this approach 'job crafting' and believes this is something many of us can do to increase our happiness at work. If you feel dissatisfied at work, consider whether you can:

Craft your attitude Can you change your attitude to your work to acknowledge the good that you do to others, or the fact that you contribute to the overall objectives of your organisation. Try writing down all the things that you do in your job that benefit

other people or the organisation that you work for. Give yourself credit for the things that you do well.

Craft your tasks How can you tweak, adapt or add to your role so that your work feels more worthwhile, to minimise the parts of the job that you dislike and maximise the parts that you do? Sometimes changing the way or time that you do things can be all it takes – for example, having set times you deal with emails rather than checking them as they come in. It can also be helpful to enlist the support of a colleague you get on well with to do this – they may have valuable insights and a more objective view.

Craft your relationships Think of ways that you can engage with coworkers, clients, or other people to build better relationships at work. Make a point of greeting people you pass when you start work. Can you suggest a social activity or volunteering opportunity that colleagues can join in with?

And if these ideas don't work, it's definitely time to find a new job. Life is too short to stay in a job you dislike. Go back to the section on finding your ikagi to help you clarify what your ideal job could be.

Money vs meaning
Does having money make you happier? US president Benjamin Franklin said: 'Money

never made a man happy yet, nor will it. The more a man has, the more he wants.' But it does seem that we need a reasonable amount of money to feel satisfied in life: the Gallup World Poll, which tracks opinion around the world, shows that people in work are happier than those who are unemployed, and that job security is a key factor in happiness. However – and this is really important – there seems to come a point when getting more money makes no different to your everyday contentment (one study put this at $75,000/£50,000 per year). Other research suggests that it's not just what you earn but how your income compares to the finances of your peers that matters. People who believe that they are paid roughly the same as their peers appear to be happier than those who feel they are comparatively underpaid.

It is of course important to have enough to cover your needs and allow you to make choices in life. But it seems that most of us recognise that money is just one aspect of our happiness. A study published in Frontiers of Psychology journal found that people would accept a salary of more than 30 percent less in order to do a job that gave them a sense of personal meaning. So, by all means, make a decent living – but don't prioritise money-making over all else. Your happiness is worth a lot, too.

Make any work day happier

Whether you are in your ideal job or not, there are plenty of ways that you can improve your daily quota of satisfaction. Here are some evidence-based ways that you can apply to most job situations and workplaces.

Have a work best friend

According to the Gallup poll, having a best friend at work is one of the biggest factors in whether you are satisfied and engaged with your job. A close friendship makes work more fun, and it also gives you a trusted ally who can help you weather challenges more easily. It can also have a significant effect on your productivity. People with a close work friendship were far more likely to say they have received praise in the previous week. So if you don't already have a good friend at work, be open to making one – extend the hand of friendship by inviting people to join you for lunch, go to work social events, and be prepared to open up about yourself rather

than keeping conversation strictly work-focused. More generally, helping out colleagues and doing mini acts of kindness can help to create a more positive and cooperative working environment that benefits both the giver and recipient. Check out page 96 for more on this.

Stop moaning

Sometimes complaining is a necessary step to creating change, but all too often it creates a bad atmosphere with no obvious benefit. Moaning about minor negative events means the brain has to relive them, according to researchers from the Eindhoven University of Technology and the University of Colorado at Boulder; they found that complaining about a negative event strengthened the memory and exaggerated its significance, which meant it lowered

mood not only at the time but the following day as well. Tolerating small inconveniences or annoyances without complaining – termed 'good sportsmanship' – on the other hand meant that negative events did not affect mood at the time or afterwards in the same way. And although the research was carried out in the workplace, it's probably a good philosophy to apply the findings to every area of life.

Do less

We can fall into the trap of thinking that to be more productive and successful we need to work more hours. This can lead us to stay late at work, work through our lunchbreaks, and labour away on tasks even when we are fatigued. But there is plenty of evidence to show that doing less can be more productive in the long run. Get in the habit of not doing

things that take up time without much effect: do you really need to go to that meeting, or read that company-wide email? Which tasks can you ditch without causing an issue?

Taking regular breaks – and in particular, taking a lunch break – can not only make you feel more productive, but increase your well-being and capacity for creativity. Breaks help us to take a step back from what we are doing, and remind ourselves of what we are trying to achieve. Allowing the mind to shift from focused activity to less structured activity can create opportunity for insights and breakthroughs – that's why we often have good ideas in the shower or when taking a walk.

Try taking a break *before* you feel zoned out. Experiment with what works for you –

many people swear by the Pomodoro technique, a popular time-management method developed in the 1980s, which recommends using a timer and dividing your work time into half-hour slots in which you work for 25 minutes, then take a 5-minute break to do something else, with a longer break every two hours. Others have found it more helpful to take a more spread-out hourly break.

Your mind will answer most questions if you learn to relax and wait for the answer.
WILLIAM S. BURROUGHS

Here are five mood-enhancing ways to take a work break:

* do a quick breathing exercise or meditation
* go for a walk
* stretch or stand up
* change your environment (even going into another room)
* doodle or do some other creative activity

And if you can't take a break, at least switch activities. Giving the brain a different type of task to focus on can be as refreshing as having a rest.

Track your wins

Most of us are future-focused at work – always thinking about the next thing we need to be doing. When we do think about what we have already achieved, we are more likely to focus on a mistake than a success. But

Three mini hacks to create a happier work environment:

Sit by the window A study at Northwestern University found that sitting in an office with windows improves your well-being and helps you sleep better at night.

Have plants nearby Researchers at the University of Exeter found that greenery in the office create a visually meditative space that boosts mood and productivity.

Introduce play Keep Lego or non-hardening modelling clay on your desk to give you a creative outlet.

it's important for your well-being to recognise your mini successes as well as the big ones. Celebrating your successes is a form of self-care, helps keep you motivated and can boost your self-esteem. So when you tick something off your to-do list, take a moment to acknowledge this. Take a breath, allow yourself to smile.

Try this: Keep a 'done' journal, in which you write down everything you have achieved, big or small. Writing up your 'done journal' can be a wonderfully self-affirming way to finish your working day that can double-up as a ritual or rite of passage that helps you to leave work behind and switch off.

Keep growing your mind

'As long as you live, keep learning how to live,' was the advice of the Roman philosopher Seneca. And there's plenty of modern evidence to show that lifelong learning is linked with well-being. Continued learning can encourage a more active life, greater social connection, and improved self-esteem, according to the UK mental health charity Mind and many other authorities.

When did you last learn something new? Children and young adults are continuously learning, but there comes a point in life when we can choose whether to learn or not. Being well educated is strongly linked to greater satisfaction in life, and many studies have found that, for older people in particular, continued learning is key to maintaining well-being and happiness. And for most of us, learning is a pleasure in itself – it makes us feel good while we are doing it, and its benefits are lasting.

Learning is a gateway to new ideas and viewpoints. When we learn something new – whatever it is – we gain in a somewhat broader view of the world. This can have a knock-on effect, making us more open to the possibility of changing the way we operate at home, in work, or in life generally. Learning allows us to keep adapting to our circumstances, which is a key part of resilience.

Learn a skill...

What would you really like to learn? When answering this question, consciously let go of preconceptions about what you are or are not good at (which are often developed at school and may not be true). Go for something that truly interests you. And don't worry whether your chosen skill is useful or not. Learning is its own reward. Here are some ideas.

A language Our understanding of the world is shaped through our first language, and learning a different one – especially one from a very different culture – can have a fundamental effect on the way you think.

An instrument Playing music is inherently enjoyable, and it seems to have a far-reaching effect on the brain, improving memory and cognitive function.

A craft Carpentry, quilting, jewellery making, soap making, DIY… crafts help bring us into the moment and give us a sense of accomplishment. Part of the reason they are so satisfying is because making things, shaping things, is such an ancient human activity: as a species, we have been fashioning clothes and whittling wood and making adornments for ourselves for tens of

thousands of years. Doing craft connects us to ancient traditions.

A life or practical skill Is there some general life skill that you have never quite got round to learning – swimming or driving or riding a bike? Or how to do first aid? Perhaps now is your time. Or perhaps a new sport such as tennis attracts you? Physical skills work the brain as well as the body.

…or a micro skill

If you don't feel you have time to learn something big, then choose some discrete small skill to master: perhaps making the perfect cup of coffee or omelette, executing a faultless three-point turn, performing a magic trick or juggling with grace, making a great fire.

Expand your knowledge

Learning is part of an attitude toward life that you can integrate into day-to-day experience. Ask yourself each evening, 'What have I learned today?' Make conscious choices to expose yourself to quality and worthwhile information. Here are several ways to keep learning:

Reading Quality books open your mind to new information and perspectives as well as relieving stress. Non-fiction gives you knowledge and, often, access to the thoughts of great minds; fiction gives you an insight to the minds of others, and can improve your empathy and emotional intelligence, according to a study published in the Journal of Research in Personality.

Listening An incredible library of podcasts is available on the internet and from broadcasters. Download podcasts and lectures of interest and listen to them on your daily commute. Audio books deliver a greater emotional impact than watching a film, according to research by University College London. And listening to quality music offers us a way of accessing other minds and inspirations, across language, time and culture.

Looking Go to art and photography and sculpture exhibitions. Great art helps to educate us, in a subtle way, about the incredible world we live in, and (like music) engages us in a constructive conversation with another sensibility. And looking at a beautiful picture or object can trigger a surge of dopamine in the brain, resulting in intense pleasure, according to scientists at University College London.

Visiting Many educational and cultural institutions run public lectures, and you'll find authors and other speakers at bookstores, libraries, local societies and the like. Search online for 'public lectures' in your nearest town or city, and see what comes up.

Deep reading

Our use of the internet and social media means that we often jump from one fact to another, taking in pieces of information in an instant without reflecting on it or making connections between different things. Similarly, we often save time by skim-reading, picking up only the pieces of information we are interested in and disregarding the rest. So-called deep reading is different. It involves slowing down, taking the time to absorb the words, engaging fully with what you are reading and reflecting on the content. Deep reading stimulates the parts of the brain that are involved in speech, hearing and vision, and so can help us become better listeners, and better at expressing ourselves when we speak or write. Literary fiction and academic books, which are likely to have rich language and complex ideas, encourage us to deep read; light fiction less so. It's much easier to deep-read when you engage with a physical paper book rather than a screen or an e-reader.

THE *happiness* TOOLKIT

Here are some proven skills
and activities that can build your
happiness quotient.

Tool one: Mindfulness

There is a wealth of evidence to demonstrate that practising mindfulness regularly can increase overall positive feelings, and also reduce levels of stress and repetitive negative thinking patterns.

Mindfulness is paying conscious attention to what is happening in the here and now without judging it. It means tuning into our experience of the moment – to what we can see, hear, feel, touch, taste, smell – rather than allowing our minds to wander from one random thought to the next. It sounds so simple, and it can be. But for most of us, most of the time, mindfulness is a skill that must be learned and practised.

Have you ever driven or walked to work, then realised that you don't remember the journey? Or been introduced to someone and instantly forgotten their name? When such things happen, it is a sign that we are not fully engaged with what is happening in the present moment. Instead we are lost in thought, generally thinking about the past or the future. When we are doing that, we are often missing out on what is going on right here, right now. That not-now-ness can take the form of regrets or wishes or worries – all states of mind that have the power to make us unhappy.

It has been estimated that our minds are wandering roughly half the time. Much of that mental meandering will be unhelpful – but at any given moment, whatever is happening, we can redirect our attention to our current experience. We can:

* be aware of what is going on in our surroundings
* be aware of what is going on in our body
* be aware of what is going on in our mind

Being aware means choosing what to pay attention to, rather than letting our mind be tugged this way and that. It means noticing the many small joys and pleasures that are part of any day (even bad days). It means – in time – developing greater awareness of ourselves and exercising more choice over the way we act, rather than merely reacting blindly.

Mindfulness is a life-changing skill. As with any skill, the more you practise, the easier it becomes. Here are some ways to bring greater mindfulness into your daily life.

1. When you wake up, take a few moments to become aware of how you are feeling. Take a deep breath in and out before you get out of bed.

Be happy for this moment. This moment is your life.

OMAR KHAYYAM

2. Whenever you walk into your home, your workplace or any other building, be aware of what you are experiencing. Notice the sounds you can hear, any aromas you can smell as well as what you can see.

3. Choose one chore a day, such as clearing the table after dinner, and challenge yourself to pay full attention to your actions while you are doing it: simply notice the feeling of the crockery in your hand, the sounds as you scrape and rinse the plates, the multitude of actions involved in simple jobs such as clearing the table.

4. Feel your feet. If you are feeling stressed, then bring your attention to the soles of your feet and their contact with the floor. Changing your focus in this way is refreshing and can shift your mood.

5. Pick a prompt for your mindfulness practice. Choose something to remind you to be aware – this could be something you wear, such as a ring or bracelet or watch, or it could be something you like to see, such as any time you notice the colour blue. Whenever you touch the ring, or see something blue, take that as a cue to come back into the now.

6. Embrace waiting. Waiting need not be tedious. Treat any time you are waiting – in a queue perhaps or at a train station – as an opportunity to practise awareness. Bring your awareness to your breathing, and allow everything else to be just as it is – including any feelings of annoyance or boredom.

Savouring

The act of savouring is similar to mindfulness, but involves actively extending and deepening your enjoyment of pleasant experiences. Savouring means slowing down. Whenever you are engaged with an activity that is enjoyable to you – having a warm shower, stroking your cat or dog, hugging a friend – allow yourself to linger and fully enjoy the experience, paying attention to all of your senses.

Savouring offers a way of combating the human tendency to derive less pleasure from experiences the longer they go on. Psychologists call this 'hedonic adaptation'. It is the familiar phenomenon whereby the last bite of a chocolate bar is usually less enjoyable than the first. One study found that wealthier people had a lower ability to savour; it's thought that having access to luxury impedes our appreciation for life's simpler pleasures.

One way to re-engage your interest and pleasure in something you do often is to abstain from it for a week. A study in which participants gave up chocolate for a week found that they appreciated it much more when they started eating it again.

Try this savouring exercise:

1. Choose a pleasurable activity and carve out 20 minutes to spend on it each day for a week. This could be visiting art galleries, going for a swim, or enjoying a walk in a beautiful place.

2. Look forward to the activity. In the same way that the run-up to Christmas, a special celebration or a party can be as enjoyable (or perhaps more so!) than the day itself, anticipating a pleasurable event allows you to access all kinds of positive emotions such as excitement and hopefulness.

3. While you are engaged in savouring, give yourself fully to the experience. Think about what is pleasurable about it and allow yourself to enjoy this. Notice any positive feelings you have – comfort, joy, interest, openness – and explore where you feel them physically in the body. Breathe deeply and allow that feeling to suffuse your entire being.

4. Relive it afterwards. Remembering good events in detail helps engender positive feelings. Savouring can boost happiness not only in the moment, but provides a good memory to retrieve later on, too.

Tool two: Mindful movement

Mindful movement is essentially exercise performed with awareness. Yoga, tai chi and other practices offer us an invitation to let go of tension and stress and to open up to a sense of calm and joy. The gentle stretches and graceful movements, when combined with deep breathing and a meditative focus, engender a sense of balance and peace.

Many of these mindful movement practices are thousands of years old, rooted in very different cultures, yet scientific research has found them highly effective in combatting modern-day stresses and in enhancing feelings of well-being.

You can bring a quality of mindfulness to any form of movement, simply by breathing deeply and focusing all your attention on the actions of your body. But learning tai chi or yoga – especially from an expert and inspiring teacher – can be a beautiful experience. By embracing these practices we can develop a new relationship with our body. We can develop greater patience as we start to respect our limitations. We begin to appreciate ourselves and our capabilities. And we can find a quietness in the mind in the moments – however fleeting – when we bring a precise mental focus to the body.

There is a large body of scientific evidence to show that mindful movement can reduce negative feelings and promote positive ones. But it is not just during and after our practice that these occur. If we make mindful movement part of our regular routine, the benefits seep into other aspects of our lives. We can see improvements in our posture, our ability to relax, our capacity for concentration, our self-esteem – all of which build our sense of happiness.

How to learn

You can learn simple movements from a book (there is an exercise overleaf) and there are online videos that can help to inspire your home practice. But taking a class is the best way to learn mindful movement, because the feedback of an experienced teacher is so helpful.

Choose your teacher with care. You want someone who has a deep and regular practice, and who has undergone lengthy training before beginning to teach. Ask friends and colleagues for recommendations, but don't treat these as gospel: try the class out and see how it feels for you. And bear in mind that you will be more likely to keep up classes if they are easy to get to, and take

place at a time that suits you. There are often classes directed at particular groups – teens, seniors etc – so keep an eye out for these if relevant. Always work at your own pace and, before you start, let the teacher know about any injuries or illnesses you have.

Which mindful movement?

Tai chi In the ancient Chinese art of tai chi, you perform a sequence of graceful rounded movements that flow seamlessly from one posture to the next. Tai chi is a martial art, performed in slow motion against an imaginary opponent, but it feels almost like a perfectly choreographed dance. Although it looks very simple, the whole body is involved in each movement and the practice develops

strength as well as suppleness. Chi gung has similar exercises that can be performed in any order rather than in the set form of tai chi. Both tai chi and chi gung can be practised at different levels and are accessible for anyone including children and seniors. There are different styles of tai chi – the Yang-style Short Form is the most popular worldwide.

Yoga There are many different types of yoga. Some forms – such as astanga and vinyasa – flow from one posture to the next, coordinating each actions with the breath. These styles can be more challenging than other types, including hatha, restorative or Scaravelli yoga, which emphasise spending longer periods in a pose to allow the body time to relax and open. Iyengar yoga emphasises attention to detail and very precise alignment. Look for what is available locally. There are also online classes; the website yogawithadriene.com offers free tutorials, including for complete beginners.

Pilates Pilates combines elements of yoga with weight training, gymnastics and breath work. It was originally developed as a form of physical rehabilitation in the 1920s, and can be a good option if you have back or other problems. The movements are very small, but incredibly effective. It is popular with dancers.

Try this: Chi gung exercise

Establish your starting posture: stand with your feet shoulder-width apart and facing directly forwards. Imagine that a string is connected to the centre of your crown and is lifting your head upwards, but keep your chin slightly tucked in.

Let your arms hang down by your sides, with your palms facing your thighs and your shoulders relaxed. Your hands should be relaxed, fingers slightly apart. Tuck in your tailbone and bend your knees slightly – almost as if you were about to sit on a high bar stool.

Alternatively, you can do the arm movements from a seated position – it's also a good exercise to do at your desk.

1. Breathe in. Slowly extend your arms away from the body and up to shoulder height. Have a feeling of them floating up, and keep your shoulders relaxed.

2. Breathe out, and bending your elbows, bring your hands in front of your chest, and then let them sink down and then back to the sides.

3. Breathe in and let the arms float up again, as in step one. Breathe out and let the arms sink down again, as in step two.

4. As you do this, imagine that your arms are moving through water rather than air – this helps you move in a slow and conscious way.

5. Breathe deeply all the way through, and keep your knees bent, your feet firmly planted on the floor, and your hands and shoulders relaxed. Repeat a few times.

Tool three: Meditation

Meditation is an ancient tradition, but it is as relevant today as it has always been. Perhaps more so, because we now know that anyone can access the healing benefits of meditation and use it to increase their overall capacity for happiness: it need not and should not be the preserve of monks and mystics, as it was thousands of years ago.

People who meditate often say that they feel more contented and less stressed, and scientists are finding that regular practice of meditation can indeed engender physical changes in the brain, leading to a better balance of positive and negative emotions. To put it simply in a few words, you can actually grow a happier brain. One study found that one effect of meditation was to reduce the size of the amygdala, the neural seat of anxiety and fear. Another found that an eight-week programme of meditation boosted activity in the left prefrontal cortex, the area of the brain that governs positive

emotions. A third study found that meditation helped increase the amount of grey matter in the precuneus, which is involved in perception; it has been found to be larger in people who believe themselves to be happy, according to a study at Kyoto University. Other research has shown that meditation reduces the amount of the stress hormone cortisol in the body after just four days of practice – and that it also relieves symptoms of depression and anxiety.

Accessing the benefits

All you need to benefit from meditation is to practise, and to practise regularly. A few minutes spent in quiet contemplation can introduce a little space into the day, allowing you to take a peaceful break from busyness and problems. As you build your ability to sit quietly, you can gain greater perspective and an increased capacity to be in the moment and experience joy.

There are indirect benefits too. Meditating regularly will increase your ability to focus. You can see meditation as an antidote to the natural scattergun approach of our mind, jumping from one thought to another. When we focus, we are more effective. And when we are more effective, we achieve more and are subsequently more satisfied with ourselves, which makes us happier. It's a virtuous circle.

Two minutes a day

If you are put off the idea of meditating or think you can't do it, try the two-minutes-a-day method for three weeks.

1. Find somewhere quiet to sit – a room where you won't be disturbed.

2. Sit on a chair, ideally one that has a firm base like a dining or office chair, with your feet flat on the floor. Set a timer to sound in two minutes.

3. Take a moment to sit up straight and take a deep breath in. When you breathe out, allow your body to relax while keeping the spine upright. You may like to do a few breaths like this.

4. Close your eyes and your mouth.

5. Breathe through your nostrils.

6. Focus on how the body moves as you breathe in and out. Notice the chest, the rib cage, the belly…

7. Don't try to make the breath deeper or slower, but let it follow its natural rhythm. Often you find the breath slows and deepens by itself, but your goal is simply to notice what is happening, not to control it.

8. When you notice that you are thinking about something other than the breath, gently direct your attention back to the breath without judging yourself.

9. Keep attending to the breath, however many times you need to re-focus, until the timer sounds.

10. Open your eyes and take a few moments before getting up.

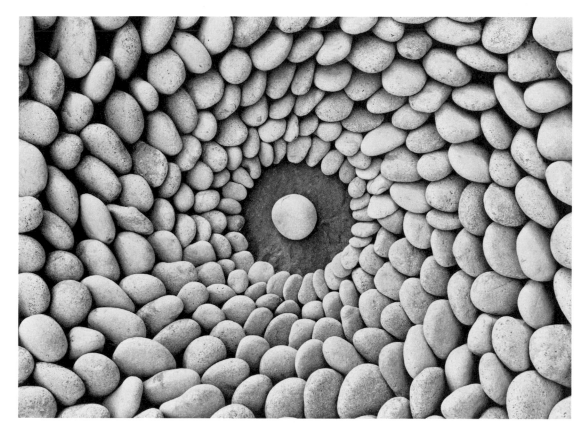

Just sitting in the moment

Once you are used to focusing on the breath, try taking two minutes to sit and be aware of all aspects of your experience in the present moment.

Start by focusing on your breath, then when your mind feels relatively steady, broaden out your awareness to encompass:

* sounds
* body sensations
* feelings
* thoughts

Keep the quality of your attention light. Allow it to be drawn to whatever aspect of your experiences seems to be predominating at that moment– perhaps an itch in the leg, birdsong or traffic noise, that thought of 'I must remember to...', or that feeling of weariness or sudden glee.

Then, once the body sensation or feeling or sound or thought fades, or another arises, let your attention shift to that.

If you notice that you have become carried away with your thoughts, then return to focus on the breath for a short period until you feel more steady... before opening out your awareness once more.

Just sitting, just being, just experiencing, for two minutes.

Deepening your practice

1. If you want to increase the time you meditate, do it gradually – to five minutes, then ten, then twenty and so on. Practise for each new time daily for three weeks before increasing it again.

2. Meditate at the same time and in the same place if you can. This helps create a sense of ritual and continuity that can help you to maintain the practice.

3. Lower your expectations. Don't think that meditating each day is a surefire route to serenity. Over time meditation can certainly help you to manage stress more easily, but the effects can be subtle and take time to become noticeable. Be patient and not goal-oriented.

4. Focus on your breath at any time of day as a way of stepping away from stress and discomfort and reconnecting with your experience of the moment.

5. Go to a mediation class. There is a quality to shared focus that inspires and strengthens your individual practice. There are many different types of meditation: the ones in this book are based on mindfulness meditation, which is non-religious (though it is based on Buddhist meditation techniques).

Meditation troubleshooting

1. If you find it hard to focus, count your breaths from one to ten – you can count the in-breath, or the out-breath. If you find you have lost count, then start from one again. Sometimes you may find you don't get above one or two for an entire practice.

2. If you lose your focus often, that can feel annoying. But how you react is more important than the fact of losing focus. Treat this as an opportunity to practise self-kindness, and just bring your attention back to the breath each time, no matter how many times your mind wanders. This is likely to happen many many times.

3. Because we are so unused to sitting quietly, observing what is going on in our own bodies, it can feel extremely tedious. Make a commitment to keep going with the practice however you feel for the three weeks. It will become more satisfying if you persevere.

4. Sitting still can also feel weirdly uncomfortable, even painful. Try to avoid fidgeting or shifting your position too often, but don't endure real discomfort. If you do need to move, do so slowly while focusing your attention on the act of moving.

5. If you have back problems and find it hard to sit upright, then lean against a wall or lie down: on your back with your legs bent and your feet flat on the floor, on your side, whatever feels comfortable. You can meditate in any position, but it's slightly harder to stay alert if you are not upright.

Tool four: Flow activities

We are happiest when we are completely immersed in what we are doing, engrossed to the point that everything else seems irrelevant. This supercharged version of mindfulness has been dubbed 'flow' by psychologist Mihaly Csikszentmihalyi, and you can apply it to almost any activity. Accessing your flow zone could be the key to increasing your happiness – and the good news is that it's simple to do.

According to Csikszentmihalyi being in a state of flow includes these elements:
* total attention on what you are doing
* clear goals, and immediate feedback
* enjoyment – what we are doing should feel rewarding
* a sense of effortlessness
* sufficient challenge, but not beyond our skills
* harmony between actions and awareness, so there is no self-consciousness
* a feeling of being in control over what we are doing

You can achieve flow in many different ways, depending on your interests and skills. A musician can get it through playing the guitar once he or she is reasonably adept; a surfer may find flow through catching the waves; someone who knits can experience it once they have learned the basic stitches. Running, gardening, writing, dancing – all these can be flow activities. Many of us find that we are most likely to experience a sense of flow at work, possibly because it can be the one place where we have to focus fully on what we are doing.

A lasting effect

Experiencing flow doesn't just feel great in the moment. It can improve your performance and creativity for days afterwards, and it also promotes lasting happiness. Because flow activities involve an element of mastery and challenge, they can feel more daunting and less immediately pleasurable than more passive activities. Researchers from Claremont Graduate University and Colorado College found that most people instinctively and correctly judged effortful activities as being more likely to lead to lasting happiness than passive ones, such as watching TV or scrolling through social media. However, they were still more likely to spend their time on the passive ones because they were the easy option. So if you want to bring more flow into your life, be prepared to put in some effort – at least initially.

Increase the flow

Here are some ways to help yourself get through the initial resistance and embrace your flow activities:

* Make time for your favourite skilled activities. Write them into your calendar or to-do list and then you will be more likely to do them.

* Clear the way. If you enjoy yoga, have the space where you do it ready-cleared, perhaps laying out your mat at night. Similarly, if you want to get up and run, sort your running clothes the night before.

* Have a transition ritual. To move from a scattered mindset to a flow activity can feel daunting, so do a calming action before you get started – taking three deep breaths in and out, for example.

* Count yourself in. Tell yourself you will count to ten and then get started. 10, 9, 8…

* Block off interruptions. You can't get in the flow if you keep getting interrupted, or if you are multitasking. Wear headphones, turn off your email, put your phone in another room. Commit to your activity utterly.

* Open your mind. Flow doesn't just come from a favourite activity. You can develop flow in any activity, from cooking to housework, meditation to cycling, if you do it with awareness.

* Reinforce your ability to focus. Do one thing each day wholeheartedly to get yourself more used to focusing. Practising mindfulness, meditation and savouring (page 62) will help.

* Know that being able to do something well often makes it enjoyable – practise!

* Keep up your interest. Once you can do your activity effortlessly, increase the level of challenge.

Tool five: Creativity

Painters and musicians are often depicted as tortured souls, but psychologists have found that making art usually makes us happier. A study of young adults by researchers in the US and New Zealand found that being creative one day increased feelings of well-being the next – and also made participants more likely to engage in creative behaviour that day too.

Do you think you aren't creative? You are. Being creative is a natural human attribute – we are being creative every time we come up with a new solution to a problem, or add a twist of our own to a recipe. Sure, our talents may differ but the need to express ourselves creatively holds true for everyone.

Being creative naturally brings us into a flow state. Because we get lost in what we are doing, we don't necessarily recognise that we feel happy at the time. But the evidence is clear: being creative also helps

us feel happier, more resilient and better at problem-solving. Psychologists believe it is part of what helps us to grow mentally and spiritually. When we create or make something, it fulfils a deep human urge to bring new things into the world. Making something is a way of giving expression to and creating order from our emotions and thoughts – of externalising our thought processes by turning them into something concrete and long-lasting. This outward-looking process can gives us a feeling of satisfaction and well-being.

If your instinct is still to say that you are no good at creating, consider whether you have ever truly dedicated time to this aspect of your life. It takes time to become skillful at doing anything – whether that is sketching or writing. Here are a few ways to fire up your creative spark:

Have a sketchbook Buy a small notebook with blank pages and carry it with you wherever you go. When you are waiting for someone or have a few minutes to spare, sketch or doodle to pass the time. Concentrate on the process rather than the result.

Try the 30 circles exercise Draw 30 small circles on a sheet of paper, then challenge yourself to turn each one into a different object – an eyeball, a wheel, a football, a face etc – in 3 minutes. Working fast stops you from editing your ideas, which stifles creativity. You can do the same exercise again, or try it with squares.

Play! Think what ways you enjoyed creating as a kid? Buy a colouring book, give origami another go, get painting, learn to juggle. Playing helps to free the mind – and it's fun for adults and teens as well as children.

Write flash fiction Write a story in under 100 words. Microfiction is intense – you don't have time to set a scene or write long descriptions so have to get straight to the point of the story. If you go over 100 words – even by a word – challenge yourself to cut it down. Make sure your title and your first and last line are immediate and arresting. Search 'flash fiction' to find online writing communities and competitions.

Bake or cook These are everyday creative outlets can give you a sense of achievement and what psychologists call 'flourishing'. Try new recipes or different ways of doing your favourite dishes.

Tool six: Journaling

You may well have kept a journal as a teenager, and then let the habit drop. But writing about yourself and your experiences is not just an adolescent phase. It has been shown to be an effective tool that can help people manage and understand their emotions better. Indeed, therapists often encourage their clients to write a personal journal.

Expressive writing of any kind acts as a creative outlet and helps to put you more in touch with your emotions. Writing is also an intellectual effort, one that requires sustained attention. In other words, to write we must organise our thoughts, and as we bring a sense of order to the page so too do we bring context and meaning to our experiences. Writing is, in short, a way of decluttering your mind.

Because journaling compels you to notice your behaviour and look on it with an honest eye, it can also help you to make positive

Fill your paper with the breathings of your heart.

WILLIAM WORDSWORTH

changes to your lifestyle. It provides a way for you to track your personal growth and achievements, and this can boost your mood. Here are some ways to make the most of journaling.

Make it a daily habit Treat your journaling time as an opportunity to reflect on your day. Do it at a regular hour if possible, choose a place to write that is cosy and comfortable, so that you want to spend time there.

Go old-style Don't make journaling yet another thing you do on a screen. Buy a beautiful book to write in and use a nice pen. Try writing extra slowly and allowing yourself to pause to think about what you want to say. Alternatively, let the words pour out: the process is a matter of personal style and preference.

And pause Take a few moments before you start writing, just to sit and breathe, allowing yourself to relax and calm your mind before you pick up a pen.

Do one sentence a day If you find it hard to keep up journal-writing, try giving yourself the discipline of writing a single sentence each day – like a handwritten tweet to your own devoted follower – you.

Or, time yourself Allocate a set period of time in which to write – even 10 minutes a day is long enough to get some words down but not so long you'll get bored.

Gamify it If the words aren't flowing, then set yourself small challenges: list five things you have eaten today, write about your best bit and your worst bit and so on.

Write from the heart Don't censor yourself, or worry about grammar or spelling. Write for yourself rather than imagining anyone else reading it. Keep your diary in a safe place so you know your words are private.

Tool seven: Thought checking

Our thoughts and feelings and actions are all interconnected. Negative thoughts can trigger negative feelings, which in turn can cause us to act in ways that do not serve us well. These feelings and actions can then feed into our thoughts and so on, creating a cycle of negativity. Becoming more aware of your thoughts, and using strategies to combat negative thinking, helps make way for greater happiness.

When we feel low, our thoughts can be repetitive and unhelpful: we may be going over and over something bad that happened in the past, as if we can somehow change its outcome; we can be worrying about the future; we may be caught in a cycle of self-blame. Our thoughts make us feel worse and also take up our time, which can undermine our attempts to make positive changes in our life. Here are some general strategies to help shift distorted or unhelpful thinking of all kinds:

1. Recognise what is going on Sometimes simply noticing a cycle of negative thinking and naming it as 'worrying' or 'blaming' or 'regretting'.

2. Question the thought Ask yourself: is this really true? Am I sure? What is my evidence? Is there another way of looking at this? Questioning the truth of what you are thinking helps keep your mind open to other possible interpretations.

3. Write or talk it out Get the thought out of your head and onto paper. Writing worries down can provide relief. Alternatively call a good friend and ask them to listen to you for five minutes.

4. Be a friend Imagine a close friend came to you with the same thoughts that you are having. What would you say to him or her? Imagine yourself talking your friend through the issue, step by step. Now compare what you would say to them, with the way you are

talking to yourself – is there any helpful reason for it to be different advice?

5. Find the compassion It's easy for us to berate ourselves for thinking negatively. But it's more helpful to be kind to ourselves, to recognise that we are feeling pain and need to take steps to look after ourselves. Use the tips on page 100 to help foster self-compassion.

6. Find a counterbalance Beat a negative with a positive. Challenge yourself to look at the situation from the reverse angle, or to find something good about the situation. For example, if you are thinking 'I am useless and have messed up at work', come up with a list of things you do well in your job.

7. Have a rest We are more prone to distorted thinking when we are tired. If you notice yourself doing it, take it as a sign that you need an early night or a siesta.

The happiness of your life depends on the quality of your thoughts: therefore, guard accordingly and take care that you entertain no notions unsuitable to virtue and reasonable nature.

MARCUS AURELIUS

8. Distract yourself Find something to do that requires you to pay attention, such as tidying a bookshelf or doing a crossword.

9. Get moving Physical activity can help refocus your attention from your thoughts to your body – try skipping, doing star jumps or going for a brisk walk somewhere beautiful. A study at Stanford University found that walking in nature helped prevent repetitive thinking in a way that walking in an urban setting did not.

10. Postpone worries One helpful technique is to designate a 'worry time' for stressful thoughts – make it specific and finite (6pm for 15 minutes, say). When they come up in your mind, tell yourself you will deal with them at the designated time.

11. STOP! Tell yourself 'Stop'. It can be helpful to visualise holding up a big STOP road sign in your mind, or imagining the red traffic light. Then distract yourself.

Recognise your patterns

Most of us are prone to particular ways of distorted thinking. These can involve exaggerated ways of thinking that don't match the reality of what is happening – but because we are so used to thinking in this way, we often don't notice when we are

being irrational. Below are some of the most common distorted thinking patterns. Read through the categories below – which ones feel most recognisable?

Emotional reasoning For example, 'I feel it so it must be true', or 'I don't feel good about the way I look so I must be ugly', or 'I am worrying that I am not good at my job, therefore I am not good at my job'. When you notice this, remind yourself that feelings aren't facts. Or challenge your thought by asking yourself, 'Am I sure about this?' or 'What is my evidence?' – and try to look at the situation more objectively.

Rule thinking We often try to make ourselves do things because we feel that we should –

'I should go to the gym', 'I must call my mum'. If you are frequently thinking in terms of what you should do, it increases feelings of resentment and guilt. If you catch yourself doing this, reword the sentence using words like 'am choosing to', or 'have decided to', which are more empowering. Or you might decide not to do this particular thing at all.

Labelling You assign a negative label such as 'useless' or 'horrible' to yourself or to someone else. But labels are a way of overgeneralising. Reframing the situation in a purely factual way, for example, 'I have said something unkind and I feel uncomfortable about it' helps to put things in perspective in a way that saying to yourself 'I am a vile person' does not.

Jumping to conclusions This is when we reach negative conclusions that are based on little evidence. For example, I *know* I'm not going to get the job' or 'Nobody is going to like me when I start secondary school.' or 'My friend thinks I am boring, that's why she has cancelled our meeting.' Remind yourself that you are guessing, or ask yourself to come up with clear evidence to justify your supposition that you can predict the future or read people's minds.

All or nothing thinking In this mode of thinking, there is no middle ground – you are, say, either brilliant or useless, successful or a complete failure. Rather than seeing in extremes, find a more realistic middle way to describe the situation. It is sure to be closer to the truth.

Filtering Here we emphasise the negative and screen out the positive. So if we have a work appraisal that is mostly positive, we will focus entirely on the two things we were told could improve. If this sounds like you, challenge yourself to remember all the positive things – as well as perhaps coming up with a strategy to tackle the not-so-good.

Disqualifying Similar to filtering, but in this case we come up with a seemingly convincing reason why the positive doesn't count; it often involves an element of mind-reading. For example, 'My boss only said the positive things because she absolutely has to say something nice about me.' You can help to counteract this tendency to disqualify the good by actively focusing on all the positive things in your life (see page 92 for tips on gratitude and appreciation).

Personalising Rather than acknowledging that very few things are entirely under our control, we think that everything that happens is about us (usually in a bad way). So if your friend has an accident, it is your fault because you were considering calling her beforehand, and she'd have stopped to chat to you instead of going out… Remind yourself that all sorts of things happen to people that aren't anything to do with you.

Catastrophising We exaggerate how terrible something is as well as its significance in our lives. For example, if we make a mistake at work, we think we are going to be sacked and then will not be able to pay the mortgage and so will lose our home. One way to deal with this is to go large: write down your absolute worst-case scenario, getting as extreme as you can. Then go back to your original worry and put it into perspective: 'I have made a mistake, but the worst that is realistically going to happen is that my manager will have a word with me.'

Overgeneralising This is a tendency to generalise, extrapolate and exaggerate, so that one bad thing is taken to mean that everything is therefore bad and/or will always be bad. For example, if you have failed your driving test, you might see it as evidence that you are simply not meant to be a driver and will never pass the test, or even that you never succeed at anything that matters to you. Overgeneralising, like all distorted thinking patterns, is usually inaccurate, so fight it both by questioning your own logic, and then by counteracting its effect by internalising other, more positive, personal statements.

QUALITIES OF *happy* PEOPLE

The mind operates like a muscle, and it can be trained to incline towards positivity and away from negativity. Here are some of the qualities and attributes of happy people, and how you can cultivate them.

Learned optimism

Optimism is linked to happiness but it is not the same thing. You could say that happiness is an emotion, while optimism is an attitude of mind, one that says things tend to work out well. Some people are natural optimists, but many psychologists believe that it is also possible to train your thinking to take a positive approach to present and future events.

You might think that a pessimist's worldview is shaped by a high incidence of unhappy events in their lives. But this is not so. Research has demonstrated that optimists and pessimists experience on average the same proportion of difficulty in their lives. The optimists are simply the people better able to deal with it. Why is this? One reason is because optimistic thinking tends to characterise negative events as temporary things that can be changed. This view makes people more inspired to keep going, to find solutions and to maintain perspective. Optimists are also less likely to blame

> *A pessimist sees the difficulty in every opportunity; an optimist sees the opportunity in every difficulty.*
>
> WINSTON CHURCHILL

themselves for their problems, and they are able to sustain a sense that things will be better in the future.

Pessimistic thinkers, on the other hand, are more likely to see difficulties as typical of their life experience. They are also likely to see their own selves as the root of problems. And of course, if you believe that something cannot be changed and is all your fault, you are more likely to allow a setback to deter you. Not surprisingly studies show that optimists are more productive, do better at work and school, are less likely to become depressed, have better relationships – even live longer. In essence, optimism expands and broadens your thinking, while pessimism narrows and diminishes it.

Here are six ways to start tipping the balance towards optimism:

1. Hang out with optimists There is a psychological phenomenon called 'neural mirroring'; it means that a good mood is contagious. Researchers at Harvard University found that if one person in a group becomes happier, those feelings can spread to their social group and then continue to ripple outwards. Take note of who is around you, and up the time you spend with positive people.

2. Reduce the negative Limit the amount of time you spend looking at the news, which tends to highlight strife and disaster. As Mark Twain advised: 'Drag your thoughts away from your troubles... by the ears, by the heels, or any way you can manage it.' Use the thought-shifting tips on page 80, practise meditation and mindfulness, get exercising or distract yourself with flow activities (see page 74). Keeping positive can be a learned craft, as well as a trait you are blessed with.

3. Play the glad game In the children's story Pollyanna, the main character is always able to come up with a positive spin on any situation. So whatever you are facing, challenge yourself to do the same. Reframing a situation can help us to feel very differently about it.

4. Appreciate what you have See the tips on page 92. Gratitude practice means that you acknowledge the positives in your life, which over time helps you to accept that there is good and bad in every day.

5. Recognise the limits You cannot micromanage every aspect of your life, however much you want to. Accepting that fact means that you can focus your energies on the things that are yours to control. Sometimes, the only thing under your control might be your attitude to a situation.

6. Be realistic! Being optimistic doesn't mean going on regardless of facts. Realistic optimists still acknowledge the negative – they just don't let it master them.

Courage and confidence

'The secret of happiness is freedom. The secret of freedom is courage.' So said the Greek thinker Thucydides. And it does seem that we need a certain amount of courage in order to feel happy, because daring to try new things is essential to an interesting and enjoyable life.

In a study at Winston-Salem State University, psychologist Rich Walker documented participants' memories of events – 30,000 reminiscences in total. He also examined 500 personal journals. The conclusion he reached, having sifted through this vast pool of autobiographical data, was that the greater the variety of experiences in a person's life, the more likely that person is to have a positive emotional attitude. Trying new things is linked to happiness. It keeps us engaged on a day to day level, and it adds richness and meaning to our lives.

Another study, this time at Cornell University, found that when we spend money on things, we quickly adapt to having them so our pleasure soon dwindles. But when we spend money on activities – going to art galleries, travelling, doing outdoor activities – the impact on our happiness tends to grow

over time because we talk about it and remember it more vividly. It's ironic that the things that last longest (material goods) have a shorter impact on us than experiences which despite lasting only in the moment actually become part of who we are.

Taking risks

It takes confidence to embrace the new. If you are confident you don't worry so much about whether you will or won't be able to do something, you just give it a go. You don't need other people's approval because you already have your own. And rather than living in what pioneering psychologist William James called 'a restricted circle of potential', you are prepared to step outside your comfort zone and take on new challenges.

What gives us confidence? Partly it's a track record of past successes: if we know we have achieved things in the past, we are more likely to try new things. Tracking your wins (see page 53) and taking time to reflect on past successes can therefore be helpful strategies to encourage yourself to be brave. Another useful approach is to adopt a beginner's mindset – you are unlikely to be brilliant at something new straight away so be prepared to start at the beginning, and don't take small setbacks personally.

The 'As If' principle

Another fantastic strategy is to act as if you already are confident – the 'as if' principle. We associate open posture with confidence – so stand tall, bring your shoulders back

When things don't go well

A study published in the Journal of Experimental Social Psychology found that reflecting on a single episode of failure can actually boost your confidence, while thinking about a whole line of failures weakens it. Bear in mind that no-one's life is an uninterrupted pageant of successes and victories. Everyone faces setbacks. Try this exercise if you are struggling to move on from one:

* Write down everything you did wrong – getting negative feelings out on paper helps you let go of them.
* Read it through once. Is there a lesson to be learned that can help you now or in the future?
* Forgive yourself. Remind yourself that you tried. And that you will be trying again, with greater knowledge.
* Once you have reflected, scrunch up the paper and get rid of it.

and your head up. This can give you a surge of empowerment. If you are engaging with other people, make sure that your face and your voice are expressive, make good eye contact and smile. It can help to visualise someone you really admire and imagine that you are tackling the situation as they would. And since we often feel more confident if we feel good about the way we look it's worth taking time on grooming and self-care.

Gratitude

A grateful attitude is known to improve feelings of happiness and well-being. It goes hand in hand with awareness, because when we practise awareness we are more likely to notice what we have to be thankful for. Conversely, when we start to practise active gratitude, we are on the lookout for positive things and thus become more aware of what we have.

Gratitude isn't something that comes easily. Most of us have what psychologists call 'negativity bias' – meaning we are more likely to pay attention to the negative than to the positive. Making an active effort to notice good things helps to put life in perspective. It can reduce feelings such as envy and regret, and strengthen our sense of optimism, empathy and resilience. Gratitude helps us savour good experiences and even improves our relationships. It makes us happier, and nicer to be around.

The most popular way to practise gratitude, as recommended by Robert Emmons, the world's leading gratitude expert and professor of psychology, is to keep a gratitude journal. The very act of writing a thought down seems to crystallise it, increasing our awareness of it. In time, gratitude writing helps us to see patterns in our experience, and become more aware of the many positives that fill our daily lives, as well as better appreciating the people who support and honour us.

Some people recommend listing three positive things about your day each evening, but studies seem to show that gratitude journaling can be more effective if done once a week – perhaps because we savour the experience more if it is less frequent. But in the end, it's not how often you write but how you write that makes a difference. Try these tips:

1. Give yourself time and space to engage fully with your writing. Treat this process as a mini-meditation.

2. Before you start writing, ask yourself 'What am I grateful for?' Try closing your eyes and placing your hand over your heart and taking a few moments to sit and breathe – just to see what comes up.

3. Write truthfully – you may not feel particularly appreciative of your relationship or your children or your job, even if you think you should be. What is it that has really been special today?

4. Think small – there can be many tiny boons in even a difficult day: a cup of tea, a warm shower, clean sheets, someone letting you through a door before them.

5. Think big – it's often said that we only appreciate things when we lose them. So allow yourself to imagine living without your health, your partner, your best friend, your home, your dog… you can write about what you most appreciate about these people or things.

6. Try to find the good. If you are finding a particular aspect of your life or person difficult at the moment, think whether there is anything you are gaining or learning from this situation or person that you can be thankful for.

7. Be expressive. Try to capture exactly what was great about the person or event or circumstance you are describing. Celebrate the intention behind a favour someone did for you as well as the favour itself. Relive the memory, allowing yourself to feel the pleasure, and recreate any sights, smells, tastes, sounds and sensations involved.

Gratitude is happiness doubled by wonder.

G.K. CHESTERTON

Other ways to practise gratitude:

Write a thank you letter Choose someone who has helped you in your life, whether you are in touch with them or not. Write a letter detailing how much you appreciate them. A study of 300 people seeking counselling found that writing one gratitude letter a week for three weeks had lasting benefits to mental health – this was true even if the letter was never sent.

Have gratitude rituals It is common in many cultures to take a few moments to appreciate the food you are about to eat. This is a lovely thing to do each and every mealtime. Extend this idea to other activities. Before you start any undertaking, give thanks for the opportunity that is before you.

Set a reminder Programme your phone to an alert sound three times a day. When you hear the sound, stop what you are doing and find something that is good about your situation at that very moment.

Count your blessings Consciously cultivate gratitude by finding one thing to appreciate in your surroundings right now. Try using the fingers of one hand to list five good things about your life.

Say thank you Actively look for opportunities to thank other people in your life. Look them in the eye and smile when you say it. Challenge yourself to say thanks to people you live with before leaving home for the day. It's so easy to take for granted the things others do for us.

Gratitude at any age

Feeling grateful can make us all happier and more satisfied with their lives, but can be especially helpful for teenagers, according to research published in The Journal of Positive Psychology. Here are some ways to help foster gratitude:

∗ Ask everyone to describe one good thing about their day at dinner. Or at bedtime, ask children to tell you about something that made them smile or feel good that day.

∗ Model gratitude by thanking your children for the things that they do.

∗ Encourage children to write thank-you notes for gifts received and for treats such as days out with grandparents.

∗ Don't buy them too much! If your children want something valuable, encourage them to earn some of the money to pay for it through doing chores.

∗ Encourage giving back. Gratitude is appreciating what we have, and we are more likely to do that if we are aware of how little others have. So – in an age-appropriate way – let children help choose charities to give money to, or where to donate toys.

Kindness

If you have ever wondered whether it is better to give or receive, the answer is clear: studies suggest that kindness leads to greater life satisfaction and happier relationships. And the reverse is also true: just as being kind can make us feel happier, being happy can make us kinder.

Giving to others involves focusing your attention outward, which can distract you from negative thoughts and increase your sense of purpose. Psychologists believe that we are hardwired for kindness, because in ancient times, cooperation was key to our survival. Kindness promotes social cohesion, it gives us the satisfaction of knowing that we have made a difference to someone else (the 'helper's high'). On a practical level, acts

of kindness and favours make it more likely that people will do something in return at some point, which can help us feel supported. And as with so many behaviours that promote survival, being kind makes us feel good: we get a boost of the love hormone oxytocin, as well as feel-good dopamine and serotonin, when we display kindness towards another.

Psychologists at the University of British Columbia found that people with anxiety experienced more positive moods after they were asked to carry out six acts of kindness a week. Another study asked employees at a company in Madrid, Spain, to do something nice for five co-workers each week. Although both receivers and givers had an initial boost in happiness, the givers reported still feeling happier than before the experiment began four months later, while the receivers had no lasting boost. Try these ways to build your kindness muscle:

Have a kindness day Choose a day a week on which you prioritise being kind; make it your theme for the day and take every opportunity that presents itself to do favours for others: let someone go ahead of you in a queue,

wave another driver through in a traffic jam, donate to a busker, take a cup of tea to your teenager…

Keep a tally A Japanese study found that people became happier and also more

grateful simply by keeping count of the kindnesses they performed in a week. Carry a small notebook with you and make a mark in it each time you do a favour, however small. You can also write in what the kindness was and reflect on how you felt about it if you have time. Look back over your notebook at the end of each week.

> *No act of kindness, however small, is ever wasted.*
>
> AESOP

Go daily Find a way to express kindness every day. Challenge yourself to act kindly towards people you don't like as well as those you do. As the ancient Greek

philosopher Plato advised more than 2,000 years ago: 'Be kind, for everyone you meet is fighting a harder battle.'

Be generous Use spare cash to buy someone else a random treat: a study by psychologist Elizabeth Dunn gave people $20 and directed them either to buy themselves something or to use it to buy a gift for another person; those who bought for others were found to experience greater happiness than those who treated themselves.

Slow down and notice. Being more aware helps you to recognise opportunities for kindness present themselves. A targeted act of kindness, such as helping someone to lift a heavy pushchair off a bus, can be more appreciated than one that is completely random, such as offering to pay a stranger's bus fare.

Bear witness Practising awareness means that you are more likely to notice others being kind. When that happens, savour the experience: witnessing acts of kindness can operate at what psychologists call a 'peak effect', a feeling of wonder and elation that can make us feel grateful to be alive; it can also remind us of the good in human beings, and make us feel more connected to those around us.

Teens and children

Parents want to make their children happy, but they are mistaken if we think giving our children everything they want will work: teaching them to be the givers has more impact on their happiness. Research from the University of British Columbia and the University of California Riverside found that 400 Canadian children were happier and also experienced greater acceptance from their peers when they carried out a daily act of kindness. So let them see you being kind; give them praise for any acts of kindness that you spot or hear about; perhaps share news of your daily acts of kindness over dinner or at bedtime; and suggest different ways to demonstrate kindness or to volunteer.

This should work for teenagers too and has the added benefit of helping them to stay out of trouble, according to a two-year study of teenagers carried out by researchers at the University of Missouri and Brigham Young University. But the study threw up an important anomaly: while teenagers who helped out their family and strangers were more likely to stay out of trouble than those who didn't, teens who directed their kindness more to their friends actually behaved worse at the end of the study – presumably because their actions were more motivated by peer pressure and a need to fit in rather than altruism. Helping children and teenagers to have self-confidence and be resilient in their friendships may help to temper this.

Self-compassion

Kindness should be directed both to ourselves and to others. There's increasing evidence to show that being self-kind correlates with lower levels of anxiety, greater resilience, and higher levels of well-being.

Self-compassion or self-kindness is different to self-esteem. Having a high self-esteem means thinking we are great – and that is a belief that can be shaken when things don't go our way. Self-compassion means thinking we are good enough as we are; it is about relating to ourselves with warmth and affection – something we can do whatever is going on in our lives. Of course, self-compassion and self-esteem are linked: if you can adopt an accepting view of yourself, then you are also likely to feel good about yourself. But whereas self-esteem tends to go up or down depending on whether things are going well for us or not, self-kindness is something that we can access and practise whatever is going on in our lives.

Self-kindness can make us more successful in achieving our goals, something that is also likely to increase our feelings of happiness. Research shows that we are more likely to stick to a habit if we forgive ourselves our slip-ups. And in a series of experiments carried out by researchers at the University of California Berkeley, participants who were encouraged to be self-compassionate after doing badly at a difficult test spent considerably longer studying for a second one than those encouraged to have high self-esteem.

Speak kindly We often speak to ourselves in a harsh and critical way, using words and a tone that we would not direct to others. When you catch yourself doing this, try to adopt a more encouraging voice. Kindness expert Kristin Neff suggests treating ourselves as we would a good friend who is suffering. You might like to take this idea further: if you have had a bad day or week, try writing yourself a short and encouraging note – as if you were addressing it to a friend. Leave it somewhere you will find it the next day and read it then.

Love your body When things are feeling difficult, stop what you are doing and connect with yourself through loving touch: rest your hands on your heart area, on your belly, or on the opposite arm as if giving yourself a hug. Take a few moments to breathe deeply as you hold yourself in this moment. Then do something nice for yourself like drinking a cup of tea or taking a short walk – anything that will improve the way you feel physically.

Soothe your mind Try doing a short meditation or breathing exercise, such as the one on page 67, to soothe a troubled mind. Or listen to some music to give your brain something to focus on other than uncomfortable thoughts. You may like to have a kindly phrase to say silently to yourself: 'it's okay' or 'I love you' as if you were a child in need of comfort. It may feel very strange or perhaps self-indulgent at first because we are unfamiliar with the concept of self-kindness. Stick with it, experimenting to see which words feel authentic and personally helpful for you.

Humour

When did you last really laugh? If you can't remember, it's time to make laughter part of your routine. As the psychologist William James once said: 'We don't laugh because we're happy. We're happy because we laugh.' And the research is clear: laughter both relaxes and energises us, and creates bonds with others.

Laughing releases a flood of endorphins into the body and decreases stress hormones such as cortisol, making us feel great. And laughter has much more of an effect on our mood and well-being than just the few moments of joy while it lasts. As well as decreasing stress, several studies have found that laughter increases our resilience to pain. It acts like a mini workout and pumps more oxygen into the blood than normal breathing, which is good for heart health and general well-being.

A study at Texas A&M University found that laughter helped increase feelings of hope. Other studies have found that more than 90 per cent of people believe lightheartedness to be helpful in dealing with stressful life events. And since we cannot think of miserable thoughts while we are laughing, humour can provide respite from repetitive thinking and give us distance from a tricky problem.

Moreover, laughing promotes positive relationships. It is perhaps no surprise that people laugh more frequently and more easily with those they like than those they dislike. But it is also true that laughing with someone helps to break down barriers and increase bonding.

Have a laugh

The positive effects of laughter seem to occur whether it is spontaneous or faked – partly because faked laughter can turn real, particularly when it is shared with others. That is the idea behind 'laughter yoga', a concept first developed by physician Dr Madan Kataria in India. There are now thousands of laughter clubs all over the world, and group laughter is a technique often used at corporate workshops as a way of dissolving hierarchies, building teamwork and encouraging creative thinking. Search online for 'laughter yoga' in your town or area to find details of a club near you, or check out Dr Kataria's laughteryoga.org. Or try this simple exercise at home:

1. Look in the mirror and smile at yourself. Say 'hello'.

2. Make your smile even broader, as broad as you can.

3. Take a deep breath in, and as you exhale, pant out a laughing sound 'ha ha ha'.

4. Repeat this a few times, making your laughing sounds louder and louder. Move your body as you do this – swaying from side to side, raising your arms above your head, bouncing up and down.

5. Keep going – it really doesn't matter if you feel silly. Stay looking at the mirror laughing, or take yourself on a mini walk around your home, laughing, moving, dancing, smiling.

6. If there's anyone else at home, get them to join in with you.

7. Go on for a few minutes – you can gradually build this up to 15 minutes or so.

8. How do you feel?

keeping CONNECTED

Good relationships keep us happier and healthier. Human beings are social creatures, so the best thing you can do to boost your happiness is to prioritise connection and community.

The friend zone

When it comes to being happy, investing time and energy into your personal connections pays dividends. Numerous studies have found that positive relationships are associated with greater happiness, better health and longer life. And happy people tend to spend less time alone than unhappy ones. Overall, it seems to be friendship that counts for most as we get older.

Having friends is the biggest predictor of day-by-day happiness for older adults. It count for even more than partners and family, according to a survey involving more than 250,000 people from almost 100 countries. The researchers suggest this may be because generally speaking we make active choices about our friendship, so by the time we are older we have learned to maintain the good ones and let go of the less-fulfilling ones.

Of course, positive partnerships and nurturing family relationships have beneficial effects on our happiness, too, but they can also involve more stress and responsibility. Time spent with our friends is, for most people and for much of the time, enjoyable and carefree.

Friendship improves happiness and abates misery by the doubling of our joy and the dividing of our grief.

MARCUS TULLIUS CICERO

Find your tribe Seeing the same group of supportive friends regularly may be the best way to bolster your happiness. In Okinawa, Japan, which is known for having one of the highest concentrations of centenarians in the world, residents have a social network called a *moai* – which can be translated as 'meeting for a common purpose'. The moai consists of a small group of friends who get together regularly, enjoy each other's company, and can be relied on for support. Psychologists have concluded that the moai along with Okinawans' strong sense of purpose (known as *ikagi*) are important factors in their happiness and longevity.

Prioritise the good Take advice from Ancient Greek philosopher Aristotle who divided friends into three categories: those who are convenient (for example, a neighbour we are friendly with or classmates at college or school), people whose company we enjoy (for example, a friend who always makes us laugh), and people who share our values and inspire us to be better people. Aristotle considered the third category to be the most lasting and useful, the most perfect kind of

friend. That is not to say that such friends never annoy or disappoint. But they are the people we turn to in crisis, the people whose company we can comfortably share without feeling a need to entertain each other or even speak.

Go face-to-face Don't let social media take the place of real-life meetings. We are physiologically programmed to need real interactions with other people. A study conducted by the University of Michigan found that our risk of depression increased as our face-to-face interactions decreased. It found that those with the lowest risk of depression were those who saw friends or family at least three times a week.

Eat communally The University of Oxford found that the more often we eat with

others, the more likely we are to feel happy and satisfied with our lives as well as with ourselves.

Factor it in If you feel too busy for socialising, then combine meeting friends with other activities such as exercising, doing yoga, or perhaps going to evening classes or craft meet-ups. Create traditions with your friends – weekends away once a year, trips to new shows at a particular art gallery, brunch on the first Sunday of the month.

Couple up If you are in a couple, then spending time with mutual friends can strengthen your relationship. We make more effort when we are in front of other people and show our best selves – and being around people who see you as a unit can help sustain you through tough times.

Talking and listening

In good relationships we can be honest and authentic. Being able to speak truthfully, and to listen well – these are skills that can strengthen our most intimate relationships but also our casual acquaintanceships. Conversation is not a competition. See it as a way of connecting and facilitating harmony rather than a verbal joust.

Learn to listen

Most of us prefer to be doing the talking rather than the listening in a conversation. When someone else is talking, we are often marking time, planning what we want to say next or thinking about something else entirely. This makes many of our conversations unsatisfying and superficial. According to one UK study there are two types of listening: 'listening to respond' and 'listening to understand'; people who 'listen to understand' were found to be more satisfied with their relationships. Here's how to go about it.

1. While the other person is talking, concentrate on being fully present. Give all your attention to this person and what they are saying.

2. You can treat this almost like a form of meditation. Breathe normally and calmly, and make good eye contact.

3. Take in their body language and gestures and tone of voice – all of which give you clues to their meaning. Be interested.

4. When it is your turn to speak, don't feel you have to respond straight away or come up with solutions. It's fine to pause to collect your thoughts. There is a time lag between hearing what someone says and processing it in your mind.

5. If you are unsure about what they have said, summarise the main points and ask if those are correct. If you want to know more, then use a counsellor's trick and ask open questions rather than those that require more than a yes/no answer. For example: 'How did that feel?' or 'When did you do that?' rather than 'Did that feel good?' or 'Was that yesterday?'

6. Then, share what you want to share in response.

Talk well

One of the wonderful things about deep listening is that having the experience of being properly heard often prompts the other person to listen better too. When you start truly listening, and making space for another person to express their thoughts, you'll often find that they begin to make space for you too. Think about what you want to say before you speak, and pay full attention to your words. Doing so allows dialogue to grow, and introduces new respect into a relationship.

Speak your truth Happy relationships contain spaces where honest self-expression can take place. Being truthful doesn't necessarily mean saying everything that enters your head, of course. Tact matters too. But the more you are able to express your truth in a calm and open way, the more you build trust and honesty in your relationships. If you cannot speak your truth, think about why. Is it you who is unable to speak it, or is the other person blocking you from doing so?

Reduce the offload Although we need to be able to talk about worries and difficulties, we don't need to recount every aspect of our day. Spending lengthy periods ranting to your partner or loved one is not conducive to a happy relationship. If work chat is getting out of hand, try restricting it to a set time – before dinner, for example – or have a couple of evenings a week when you don't talk about work at all.

Be kind Bring a quality of kindness to your words and also to your tone of voice. Whether speaking to your partner, your mother, your best friend or an acquaintance, make a decision to speak softly. Don't use aggressive forms of speech such as mockery, blame, gossip, sarcasm, or expressions of irritation or contempt. Try challenging yourself to speak with kindness for 24 hours – it's harder than you think.

Note how you feel When you talk (and also when you listen), be aware of how you are feeling. When we say (or hear) things that make us uncomfortable, we can have a physical response such as tension in the belly or constriction in the throat. If you notice this, see it as a cue to take a deep breath rather than coming back with a hurried, instinctual response.

Know your timing People aren't always ready to hear what you want to say, of course. A difficult or deep conversation may not be appropriate if you are in public, or too tired, or if there are other things going on. Sometimes you may need to choose the right moment. And sometimes, you will not be listened to even if what you say is important. Be aware of the vibes, and pick your time and place.

Strategies for happier relationships

When psychologist John Gottman conducted research into how couples interact, he found that the secret of a happy marriage could be summed up in a 'magic ratio': for every negative interaction, there were at least five positive ones.

We can probably apply this principle to all our personal relationships: think, if you have recently vented to your best friend, have you also had five positive interactions? If not, set yourself the task of creating those moments. Here are some of the best ways to bring positivity into your relationships.

Promote growth We know that purpose is central to our overall happiness. The happiest relationships are those in which we

facilitate the other person's purpose and passion – and they facilitate ours. For couples, shared interests are less important than a shared awareness that both partners are entitled to follow their dreams.

Pay compliments Have you said something nice to your loved one today? Compliments introduce positivity into our interactions – so long as they are timely and sincere. A Japanese study found that receiving a compliment activated the same part of the brain (the striatum) as did receiving a cash reward. And it's just as important to be able to take a compliment well: when someone says something nice to you, smile and say thanks rather than dismissing it – be gracious.

Express appreciation The people who do most for us are often those we least appreciate. If your partner makes you tea every morning, it's easy to take this for granted. Active gratitude is a way of staying aware of the kindnesses that we are shown. When we express appreciation for the little everyday things that a partner does for us, this increases feelings of connection and relationship satisfaction, not only for the

recipient but for the person doing the good deed, according to a study by researchers at the University of North Carolina.

Enjoy the good Couples who are able to celebrate each other's successes report being more satisfied in their relationship, according to a study at the University of California. Researchers found that sharing happiness in positive events counted for more than commiserating when things went wrong. And the good in the past is as important as the successes of the present. Sharing joy in things that happened in the past, last week or a decade ago, is one of the ways in which we build stronger bonds with others, according to other research.

Keep laughing A good sense of humour is a kind of fast-track to a happy state of mind. It is also an indicator of positive relationships: couples who share a laugh are more likely to stay together, say researchers at the University of Kansas. The fact is: there is an amusing angle to most life situations. When you miss the last train, step in a deep puddle, embarrass yourself at a job interview, it's not really tragic; it's actually kind of funny – as you will realise if you imagine yourself telling the story later.

Just be there If you do one thing to improve your relationships, it is this: simply gift the other person your full attention – no phones, no distraction, just your true presence.

Loving touch

Touch seems to fulfil a primal need. Research has found that physical contact bonds relationships, and fosters gratitude and trust. We know this instinctively: it's why we hug a child who is hurt, shake hands or kiss in greeting, pat the back of someone who is upset or grieving. Touch, used appropriately, is a way of saying: I feel you, and I feel what you are feeling.

With acquaintances Try bringing warm – when appropriate – touch into your encounters. Touching a person on the arm increases the likelihood that they will help you. One education-based study found that a student who received a brief touch to the back or arm was more likely to volunteer in class than one who didn't.

Therapeutic touch Regular massage or other forms of therapeutic touch also increases feelgood chemicals in the body. Tiffany Field, director of the University of Miami's Touch Institute, carried out a number of experiments to show the significance of

touch: in one trial, elderly people received social visits that either did or didn't include massage; the group who had massages received more emotional benefits than those whose visits were purely social. At any age, having massages or touch therapies such as acupressure or zero balancing (which uses physical touch to release held emotions in the body) is a wonderful form of self-care.

Give us a hug Penn State University researchers instructed a group of students to give five hugs a day for a month – they had to hug as many different people as possible. At the end of the experiment, the huggers reported feeling much happier than a control group who were instructed to read. And other research found that a long hug – ones that last at least 20 seconds – triggers the release of the 'love hormone' oxytocin, which calms the nervous system and promotes feelings of connection. So…

1. Introduce the idea of the 20-second hug to your loved ones. Ask them to try it as an experiment – or if it feels right simply lengthen the time you spend in a cuddle.

2. Stand and hold each other in a full-body hug while you each count silently to 20, or if you prefer, for the length of time it takes you to have three deep breaths.

3. Allow yourselves to melt into the embrace, as if this is all that matters in this moment. Everything else can wait while you experience the time of connection.

4. Come apart gently.

Hand to hand Holding hands with children or partners is a very clear symbol of togetherness. And the physical connection helps to reduce stress and increase feeling of relaxation. It can minimise nervousness before a stressful event, such as public speaking, and even lessen the perception of pain. A study in which married women were subjected to uncomfortable heat found that they felt less pain when asked to hold their husband's hand.

Romantic touch Touch is central to happy romantic relationships, and affection is as important as sex. One study asked people to kiss more often and for longer over six weeks; it found that participants completing the challenge reported higher levels of satisfaction in their relationship and also said they were less stressed. Experiments conducted by Tiffany Field found that pregnant women who were regularly massaged by their partners were less anxious and more settled.

Too often we underestimate the power of a touch, a smile, a kind word, a listening ear... or the smallest act of caring, all of which have the potential to turn a life around.

LEO BUSCAGLIA

Embrace community

A sense of belonging has a huge effect on how happy we feel, and also how healthy we are. Building social connections is something that all of us can do. Whether we are married, partnered up or single, have a busy social life or not, we can make a connection within the wider world, and through that link find greater feelings of happiness.

There is plenty of research to show that social connectedness has a positive effect on our mental health, and increases our sense of happiness. Having a human network has also been found to ease stress in life transitions, such as retirement or, say, starting university. It is a key factor in healthy aging for older adults and in promoting positive mental health in teenagers. It can also help to mitigate symptoms of depression.

One study from Nottingham Trent University found that people who felt that they belonged to a group were more

satisfied with life, and had a stronger sense of purpose than those who didn't. And the more groups people belonged to, the greater the cumulative effect on the individual. The researchers said that each separate group represented an additional nine per cent boost in happiness.

Group work

Working together can increase feelings of meaning in our lives, because groups can facilitate shared purpose. They can in fact bolster our sense of self, because a group brings us into contact with other people who share our vision and values. They help promote companionship and enjoyment, offer us opportunity to learn new skills and gain greater knowledge, and be a source of support during difficult times.

Sign up, sign in

We can find a sense of well-being in any group to which we belong, so long as it reflects our interests and values. The family automatically operates as a group, but so do clusters such hobby and interest circles, sports teams, churches and other faith communities.

Take a sheet of paper and write down any and every group you belong to. Consider whether these reflect your values and interests. If not, then ask yourself if there is a group that you do think you want to be part of. Here are some ideas:

Community groups Could you join or start an initiative in your local area? To best foster a sense of belonging, choose groups that meet regularly rather than helping with one-off events.

Political groups Is there a cause that matters to you, or a political party that reflects your beliefs? Might you benefit from working for a cause with like-minded people?

Spiritual groups It may be that you subscribe to a recognised religion that gives you a

sense of belonging, but there are other options such as meditation groups.

Professional groups Is there a society connected to your work that appeals, for example: a union or an association? Or something like an alumni society for your school, college or university?

Identity groups There may be a group specifically connected to your sense of identity, for example, single parents or LGBTQ+.

Hobby groups Whatever your interest, there is likely to be an organised group enjoying it too, whether trainspotting, singing, photography, surfing, real ale or origami.

Activity groups Rugby, yoga, lindy hop, parkrunning – there is a group near you. Team sports and dance are particularly good because they encourage social interaction as well as health-promoting exercise.

Educational groups Is there a library, a heritage home, a local history society or a genealogical community that you could draw on or contribute to? Research it: there may well be something around the corner.

Volunteering

Unpaid work might seem an unlikely route to happiness, but volunteering has consistently been shown to offer a host of benefits to the giver. Human beings are nicer than we think.

Why volunteering is conducive to happiness:

* It is one of the ways in which we can make a difference. That is to say: it creates purpose in our lives.

* It connects us to something bigger than ourselves.

* It usually involves contact with others – and that provides a invaluable sense of social integration.

* Doing good for others gives us a natural chemical shot of endorphins – what psychologists call the 'helper's high'.

Interestingly, a study published in the BMJ Open journal found that volunteering seems to have most benefits for people over 40. This may be because younger people feel they need to volunteer for the sake of their cv or careers while after a certain age we no longer feel that we are doing what we do for our own advancement: middle-age altruism is a simpler and purer proposition. The happiness benefits of volunteering have been shown to be higher if you do it weekly at least, but less-regular volunteering is also

beneficial to the person doing it. It's important to think about what you can manage – taking on too much or trying to fit volunteering into an already stretched life could be counterproductive. If you know this is the case, you might find it easier to help out on an occasional basis rather than take on a more regular commitment. Respect your own limits.

> *How wonderful it is that nobody need wait a single moment before starting to improve the world.*
>
> ANNE FRANK

You are likely to get the most benefit if you volunteer in a way that suits what you enjoy and believe in. Drop any thoughts or feelings about what you 'should' do, and do something that pleases and nurtures you. If you enjoy gardening, then volunteering to help keep up the grounds of a hospice or community park could be enjoyable. If you find talking to people satisfying, then volunteering for a befriending charity in which you visit someone who has difficulty getting out and about could be more your thing.

Giving money

To give money away makes us happy, too. A study by Harvard professor Michael Norton found that spending money on other people made us happier than spending it on ourselves (see also pages 48–49). Other research has found a strong correlation between charitable giving and happiness – and this holds true in both rich and poor countries. Researchers studying activity in the brain found that giving to charity activates the reward area of the brain in the same way as having sex or eating chocolate.

And giving also seems to ward off feelings of depression. The University of Michigan's Panel Study of Income Dynamics, which polls thousands of US citizens, found that people who gave money away were 68 percent less likely to say they had felt 'hopeless' at the end of the year, and 34 percent less likely to say they had 'felt so sad nothing could cheer them up'.

Make the most of your giving:

✳ Select organisations that you feel passionate about. Choose charities that align with your values.

✳ Find out where your money is going. We get more joy from giving to specific projects that allow us to track the positive effect of our donations.

✳ Give little and often. You'll get more of a boost than giving a single larger chunk of money.

✳ Keep track of the work the charity does, so that you feel personally involved.

✳ Don't donate in order to get some other benefit – such as a free t-shirt or entry into a prize draw. Any sense that there might be an ulterior motive makes giving less satisfying.

✳ And don't donate simply because you feel guilty. Give where you want to, freely and with an open heart, even if it doesn't fit with what others think you should do.

Feel the interconnection

One of the things that can make us feel unhappy is a sense of separatedness and isolation from others. And when we are feeling low, we often seek to isolate ourselves, turning away from loved ones and sources of support. These three exercises offer some gentle ways for you to open up to a greater sense of community and interconnection.

Experiment 1: Go for a walk

Go for a 15-minute walk, and as you walk, be on the lookout for signs of how other people might be making life better for us all.

∗ As you walk, say, through a park or town square, notice different aspects of the environment and reflect on the people that have built or designed them, the people who maintain them, the people who use them: for example, the flowerbeds and how they have been tended; the roads and the people who laid them… every detail of our environment is a product of people working together. Walk slowly, and pause from time to time.

∗ Be aware of positive interactions between the people that you pass – the person holding a child's hand, the man waving at a friend across the road, that bus driver

opening the doors for the passengers. Notice how people are going about their business, doing what needs to be done, often helping each other in almost unnoticeable ways.

∗ Open up to the difficulties that others face – the elderly person walking with a stick, someone sleeping in a doorway, a harassed parent. Avoid the compulsion to judge or solve, and simply allow yourself to be aware of the human experience that is taking place before you.

∗ Take some quiet time at the end of your walk to reflect. Sometimes, simply allowing ourselves to notice others can endow us with a sense of compassion, a feeling that we are all in this world together. This feeling of connection can help alleviate any sense of loneliness.

Experiment 2: Talk to strangers

Hate commuting? Next time you are on a journey, set yourself the challenge of exchanging a comment with another person. a stranger, however briefly. When commuters were challenged to do this by researchers at the University of Chicago, the ones who spoke to a stranger reported having a more pleasurable experience than those who kept themselves to themselves. Interestingly when people were asked about the experiment beforehand, they incorrectly predicted that the group charged with engaging with others would have the least pleasurable experience, and that the solitary group would enjoy their experience the most. These unjustified fears seems to demonstrate that we long for personal interaction more than we realise.

Experiment 3: Be a well-wisher

This loving-kindness meditation, drawn from Buddhism, can help to melt away a sense of division and promote feelings of social connection, and friendliness towards one's fellow human beings.

It involves repeating set phrases of goodwill and, crucially, it doesn't matter whether you actually feel the goodwill at the time. Try to allow whatever feelings come up just to be there, without judging yourself for them or trying to change them.

Practised regularly, the loving-kindness meditation can increase positive emotions, but even a single session can help us to feel more connected to those around us.

✳ Sit in a comfortable but upright position, and close your eyes.

✳ Breathe deeply for a period until you feel ready to start.

✳ Gently say the words to yourself: 'May I be safe and happy; may I be healthy; may I live in the world with ease'. Repeat, allowing the good wishes to resonate through you.

✳ Think of someone you care for deeply. Repeat the words as if saying them to this person: 'May you be safe and happy; may you be healthy; may you live in the world with ease'.

✳ Think of someone you don't much like. Apply the same words to him or her: 'May you be safe and happy; may you be healthy; may you live in the world with ease'.

✳ Think of a group to which you belong – your family, a friendship group, a class you go to. Direct these words to the whole group, including yourself: 'May we be safe and happy; may we be healthy; may we live in the world with ease'. Encompass everyone in the group in your good wishes

– those you like, those you dislike, those you feel neutral about.

✳ Now imagine these words encompassing a larger group – your community or your town – and repeat them once more.

✳ Now expand the group to encompass your country and the world, including all living creatures in your thoughts. 'May we all be safe and happy; may we all be healthy; may we all live in the world with ease.'

✳ Let go of the need to repeat the phrases but stay sitting, breathing deeply, for a short period before opening your eyes. Note how you feel without judgement or expectation. Then take some deep breaths before opening your eyes.

Index